*A*ttorney ASK AN

All About
FLORIDA LAW

By
Joseph F. Pippen Jr.
Attorney, Writer, Educator

Book Order Dept.
FLA. 1-800-432-0399
U.S. 1-800-327-7055

ISBN 0-913455-05-9

Linch Publishing, Inc.
Box 75
Orlando, FL 32802

This book is intended to answer the most often asked questions concerning legal issues. This book is not intended as a substitute for legal counsel and questions will be answered in a general context. Specific legal questions usually have too many variables to give concise, legal answers covering all ramifications.

Book Order Dept.
FLA. 1-800-432-0399
U.S. 1-800-327-7055

ISBN 0-913455-05-9

ABOUT THE AUTHOR

JOSEPH FRANKLIN PIPPEN, JR.—Attorney, was born in 1947 in Richmond, Virginia. He graduated from Virginia Tech in 1969 with a degree in economics. He also served in the National Guard as a Captain of a Combat Engineering Group. From 1969 until 1980 he was an executive with his management positions including manufacturing, production control, marketing, purchasing, finance and public relations.

From 1980 through part of 1982 Joe Pippen served as general manager of Micro-Plate, Inc. of Florida and helped guide the small, high-technology company into a major force in the printed circuit-board industry.

Joe Pippen graduated from the University of Baltimore Law School in 1975 with a Juris Doctorate and has been a sole practitioner with a general practice of law since 1982. He has also taught Business Law and Management at Anne Anundel Community College and at St. Petersburg Junior College.

Besides his noteworthy business and career achievements, Pippen has numerous other achievements to his credit. He has been honored four times as one of the "Outstanding Men of America," has been listed in *Who's Who in Finance and Industry*, has been named as one of the "Ten Outstanding Young Men in Maryland," and "Outstanding Jaycee of the Year" in Maryland. He also has been cited by the Governor of Maryland as one of the "Outstanding Volunteer Activists." The volunteer achievements he is most proud of are the millions of dollars he has raised for the United Way and his volunteer role with young people and the free enterprise system through the Hugh O'Brien Youth Foundation.

Pippen is a noted speaker and lecturer on motivational and personal dynamic subjects as well as management and legal topics. His weekly column, "Ask an Attorney," appears in several local newspapers, and can be heard weekly on WPLP (57 AM) Radio, as talk host of "Ask An Attorney."

He is married to his high school sweetheart, Beverly, and they have two sons, Trey and Troy. The presently reside in Largo, Florida.

DEDICATION

I dedicate this book to my loving wife Beverly who has supported and assisted me in all my endeavors with love and dedication.

ASK AN ATTORNEY

by
Joseph F. Pippen

CONTENTS

ATTORNEYS

CHOOSING AN ATTORNEY

Q. *How would a new Florida resident choose an attorney?*

A. There are many methods available for you to choose a new attorney. Some choices would be:

1. Ask friends, neighbors or co-workers about lawyers they have used and with whom they have had successful experiences.
2. Contact your state, city or county bar association and ask for the names and phone numbers of attorneys who handle cases within your needs. The Florida Bar also has a statewide Lawyer Referral Service which can be reached by calling 1-800-342-8011.
3. Many attorneys advertise in the yellow pages and/or newspapers. These ads often state their specialties, office hours and location.
4. If you live near a law school you may wish to contact the dean's office or law professors for a recommendation.

Some questions you may wish to ask the attorney at or before the initial meeting are as follows:

1. Is there a charge for the initial consultation? Many attorneys do not charge for the initial meeting.
2. Ask the attorney what percentage of his or her practice is devoted to cases like yours. Many attorneys can handle a variety of legal matters, while others devote most of their time to one area.
3. You may wish to ask the attorney for references from past similar cases. This information may or may not be available as most attorneys may be very hesitant to release client names for ethical reasons.
4. Ask the attorney if he or she will personally work on your case or delegate it to others.
5. You should also make sure you understanding the billing arrangements, how progress reports are made to you regarding your case and how long the attorney estimates your case will take to process.
6. Attorney fees are negotiable and should be a factor in making your decision. Some attorneys charge flat fees, others charge hourly rates, and others take retainers or work on a contingency basis. The hourly rate could vary a great deal from attorney to attorney. Whatever fee arrangement you ultimately decide upon it is best that it be in writing. The writing could also provide a written estimate of the costs and how bills would be itemized.

Remember, when you choose an attorney, you could be choosing an advisor, confidant, and possible a friend for life—GOOD LUCK!

RESIDENCY

ESTABLISHING RESIDENCY

Q. *How can I establish residency in the State of Florida?*

A. There are many reasons for wanting to establish Florida as your legal residence, especially tax-saving reasons. Some of the ways to establish Florida as your residence are as follows:

(a) File a Florida Declaration of Domicile and Citizenship at the county courthouse;

(b) Register to vote in Florida and cancel your previous voter's registration;

(c) Have a Will or Living Trust prepared that states Florida as your domicile. Under certain circumstances, the personal representative in your Will must be a Florida resident.

(d) Open a bank or securities account in Florida and have monies or securities transferred to that account;

(e) Obtain a Florida drivers permit and Florida license plates for your car, discarding any you may have had previously;

(f) Use your Florida address on all legal documents including leases, cars, contracts, etc. and have your mailing address changed to Florida;

(g) If you are buying or have bought a Florida home, then apply for the Florida homestead exemption;

(h) Transfer all of your local and religious organization memberships to local Florida groups;

(i) Apply for credit cards using a Florida address and secure Florida lines of credit;

(j) File a state intangible personal property tax return each year, if it is applicable to your particular case;

(k) Use your Florida address when you file your federal income tax returns.

Q. *If I spend part of the year in Florida and part in Maryland but I die in Florida what state would be determined to have been my residence?*

A. The courts will analyze all of the facts and determine the location of your permanent residence. Answers (a) through (k) above will be crucial in determining your residency. Generally speaking, Florida offers more tax benefits than other states.

If you were determined to be a Maryland resident and you died in Florida with a Maryland Will (or no Will), then your estate would be probated in Maryland. If any Florida real property was involved, that portion of the Will would have to pass through the Florida probate court.

DUAL RESIDENCES

Q. *Can two states claim you as a resident for tax purposes if you live in two states part of the year?*

A. You should take all steps possible to avoid a claim of dual domicile upon death. You should analyze the tax structure of both states and decide where you want to live. You may wish to consider changing the situs of assets by changing their character.

Real estate, tangible personal property, and mineral interests are generally governed and taxed upon death only in the state where the property is located. Intangible property, e.g. securities and partnership interest, are usually subject to taxation, if any, in the state of the owner's domicile. Transferring real estate into a corporation, partnership, or certain types of Trusts may change the nature of the property from real property to tangible property.

Usually, real property can only be taxed at its situs, whereas cash, bank accounts and securities (intangible property) are taxed where the decedent was domiciled at the time of death.

The United States Supreme Court has ruled that the question of domicile is for the states to decide, and it is not unconstitutional for more than one state to claim a decedent of that state for the purpose of imposing an inheritance tax. Because domicile is determined under each state's law, two or more states can constitutionally tax a person's intangible property.

To constitute a domicile, or to effect a change of domicile, there must appear both an actual residence and an intention to remain there or make it one's home. The intention to establish a residence must be bona fide and unequivocal. If one were to live in Florida for five to seven months and live in another state for the remainder of the year, the determination of where he was domiciled would depend on some or all of the following factors:

1. Whether residence was declared homestead;
2. Location of personal property;
3. Location of voter registration;
4. Location of banking accounts;
5. Membership in clubs, churches, etc.;
6. Location of charge accounts;
7. Location of securities;
8. Place where Will or Trust was signed;
9. Address on tax returns;
10. Address of automobile license;
11. Subscriptions;
12. Telephone listings;
13. Location of contributions.

Assets in multiple states may also have to go through multiple probate proceedings. Your attorney may advise you how these assets can avoid probate.

WILLS & ESTATE MATTERS

WILLS

Q. *What happens if I die without a Will?*

A. The state of Florida will "in essence" make out a Will for you. Generally speaking the laws of the State of Florida are very general and practically never could carry out your precise intentions or desires without your planning your own Will.

Further, the court will appoint a personal representative to handle your affairs and this person might be a senior family member regardless of experience in estate management. The lack of a Will could cost thousands of dollars because of the lack of proper estate planning.

The bottom line to this question is that Wills are relatively inexpensive—starting at $25.00 and everyone should see their attorney regarding getting one prepared.

Q. *What are the Advantages of a Will?*

A. A Will provides for the individual needs of your family members. You decide who, what, when and where. You may decide to spread the payments out over a long period of time, or provide for the college education of a grandchild or niece. You may remember a church or favorite charity.

By planning your estate you may avoid certain tax burdens by creating Trusts in your Will.

A primary consideration is that persons who die without Wills have their estates tied up for long periods of time and loved ones are often not even able to liquidate necessary assets to pay funeral expenses.

As mentioned before, Wills are very inexpensive in relationship to the problems caused by not having one.

Q. *Are Wills Revocable and How Often Should They be Reviewed?*

A. Yes. Wills are revocable and can be changed at any time for any reason. Wills should be reviewed periodically or when individual circumstances change. The following are examples or changes:

(a) Recent changes in federal or state laws make it necessary for everyone to review their Will if they have not done so in the last 24 months.
(b) Substantial changes in assets or ownership in various businesses require review and tax planning.
(c) If you have relocated to Florida your Will should be reviewed.
(d) Deaths, births, or marriages which have changed the circumstances of your original intentions.

Wills may either be rewritten or may be amended inexpensively by adding a codicil.

Most people put off having a Will prepared because they don't like thinking about death. Wills are an effective, inexpensive and expeditious way of protecting your family and loved ones and insuring them of an uncomplicated distribution of your estate at the time of death.

WILLS

Q. *Is My Out-of-State Will Valid in Florida?*

A. Your out-of-state Will is probably valid in Florida if it was executed properly. It must also meet certain requirements especially if the personal representative is a non-resident of Florida. Under certain conditions, out-of-state witnesses to the Will must be brought to Florida or a court proceeding must be initiated in the other state.

Florida now utilizes the "self-proving" Will. This simply means that if the Will is notarized when executed, the witnesses are not required to appear in court.

Q. *Who can Serve as a Personal Representative in Florida?*

A. Any Florida resident who is 18 years of age or older, of sound mind and not a convicted felon may serve as a personal representative. A non-resident of Florida must meet these requirements:

(a) A legally adopted child or adopted parent of the decedent;

(b) A blood relative of the decedent; or

(c) A spouse of a person otherwise qualified to serve.

Q. *What are the Duties that may be Required of a Personal Representative?*

A. The potential duties of a personal representative are too numerous to mention in this column. Generally, they may be broken into five categories:

(a) Collect assets and information including locating and assembling names, addresses, heirs, deeds, personal belongings, insurance information, etc.

(b) Determine debts and claims against the estate including analyzing current bills, legal publication regarding claims against the estate, analyzing insurance, mortgage and loans concerning the estate.

(c) Managing the estate. This includes setting up bookkeeping of estate, re-registering stocks and bonds, reviewing investments, and supervising family business until decisions can be made concerning status of business.

(d) Determine and pay all taxes including all tax returns, such as inheritance, federal, property and personal taxes concerning the estate.

(e) Distributing the estate. This final phase normally calls for decisions such as selling assets to raise cash for specific legacies, paying all final costs and preparing final, detailed account for the court.

CONTRACT WILLS, JOINT AND MUTUAL WILLS

Q. *Please explain contract Wills, joint Wills and mutual Wills.*

A. Two related individuals may make a contract to make a mutual Will or a joint Will.

A *Joint Will* is a single Will, jointly signed and generally signed by two or more people, often devising property held as joint tenants or tenants by the entireties. The problem with a joint Will is that the original Will has to be filed, and when the first party dies, the second party does not have an original Will to file.

A *Mutual Will* is generally used to refer to Wills in which the testators name each other as beneficiaries or execute their Will at the same time with the common intention of leaving everything to one another.

All mutual and joint Wills are revocable and if one party decides to revoke a Will and prepare another, then his *last* Will would be the one that is effective. As the old saying goes, "Your last Will is your last Will."

When parties "contract" to Will, that is, sign an agreement to execute mutual Wills, leaving everything to one another, the Will may still be revoked and a new Will may be executed that will be considered the last Will in court. The remedy that one has is not against the Will in this case but on the "contract" agreeing to make the mutual Will.

The most common problem arises when husband and wife are each married for the second time and both have children from the first marriage. The common concern is generally from the husband, as statistics show that the husband dies first. His concern is well founded because if he dies first, leaving everything to his wife, then his wife can leave everything to her children. His children would receive nothing, in this example.

Often, there is such a great deal of trust between husband and wife that they trust one another to do the right thing and make no provision and have no estate plan for the future.

Unfortunately, the unthought of scenarios often happens:

FIRST SCENARIO:
Husband dies leaving everything to wife. Wife becomes senile and comes under the control of her oldest son. Son manipulates mother's estate so that he

9

receives everything (he is her only child) and husband's children from a previous marriage, receive nothing.

SECOND SCENARIO:

Husband dies leaving everything to wife. Wife remarries, creating new Will leaving everything to husband No. 2. Wife dies. Neither husband No. 1's children or wife's children would receive any part of the estate in this example.

There are several estate planning tactics that can be taken to protect your estate for those you love. See you local attorney to have your plan implemented or reviewed.

POOR MAN'S WILL

Q. *Why has joint tenancy been called the "Poor Man's Will" or "poor man's trap"?*

A. Joint tenancy has long been considered by many people as a reason not to have a Will or a Trust. The common misconception is that if everything is held jointly with rights of survivorship that the estate will avoid probate and there is no need for a Will or estate planning. Such planning is filled with several traps.

"JOINT OWNERSHIP WITH A SPOUSE" Joint ownership with a spouse does, in fact, avoid probate in some cases, but several traps are present. If both spouses die at the same time, the Will of the spouse who was determined to have died last, would be the one which would be probated. Thus, joint tenancy would not have avoided probate.

If one spouse dies and the surviving spouse goes through a period of depression, inactivity, and fails to take estate planning steps, then probate and taxes could result. In some cases where incompetency occurs, joint tenancy will result in a guardianship having to be instituted before select assets can be sold. Joint ownership with a spouse could also lead to excessive estate taxes in the larger estates because of a failure to properly plan.

"JOINT OWNERSHIP WITH A CHILD" Joint ownership with adult children is filled with problems. For example, just last week a widow told me, "My husband died several years ago and because of my depression and concern about what to do I placed my assets jointly in an account with my son. He was also depressed and in a matter of months he had lost my entire estate while gambling." In another case, a grieving widower placed everything in joint names with a loving daughter. The daughter was involved in a car accident in which she was at fault. Some of her mother's assets were lost because the daughter was considered a part owner of the assets. In other cases parents place assets in a joint account with a child and the child goes through a bitter divorce. Because the child is part owner of the assets, claims are made against them.

As you can determine from the examples, joint ownership with children is not always a good estate planning device and sometimes deserves its name, "poor man's traps."

"IN TRUST FOR" "In Trust for" accounts and "Totten" Trusts have also been referred to as "Poor Man's Wills." These arrangements are really miniature Trusts and pass to the party for which they are held upon the death of the originator of the account. If the originator becomes incapacitated, the account could come under the supervision of the guardianship court.

Many estate planning techniques can be used to avoid the pitfalls of the "Poor Man's Will" or "poor man's trap." Consult your local attorney.

VIDEO WILLS

Q. *Are video Wills valid*

A. Video Wills (with audio) are not valid by themselves as the State of Florida requires that Wills be in writing. Video Wills have become useful tools as a supplement and are occasionally recommended when:

1. Proof may be needed to show that the testator actually signed the Will with his signature or mark and that it was properly witnessed;
2. Video sometimes can be excellent proof that the testator had testamentary capacity to execute the document. During the signing of the Will the testator can acknowledge what he is signing and that he understands the effect of what he is doing. The video can also be used to show that the testator knew the extent of his property. Often a video may show the testator reciting the type and description of his property.
3. When certain family members are omitted from the Will, the testator may make verbal statements on video explaining why these decisions were made. Sometimes family members are discouraged from contesting the Will when this type of evidence exists.
4. Video can be used to show the lack of undue influence or fraud. With the testator explaining why decisions were made in his own words and that these decisions were made as a result of his own free will, then Will contests due to undue influence and fraud are less likely.
5. Video Wills can be helpful to interpret clauses in the written Will if disputes arise. The testator can describe what he meant regarding distribution of his estate in his own words.

However, video Wills are not without possible problems. In some cases the testator may appear to be incompetent even though he is not. Some testators give extremely poor appearances or have a negative bias which may have a negative impact on certain jurors. Video cameras may be used so that the image recorded is misleading or distorted and may not be the best evidence to prove the testator's intent.

Another concern is that video Wills may be altered. Proper steps may be taken to store the tape away from magnetic fields, high temperature and high humidity as well as away from those who would like to alter or destroy the tape.

Video may be used for the distribution clause of a Living Trust or other form of Trust just as easily as it can be for a Will.

POUR-OVER WILLS

Q. *If I have a Living Trust, do I still need a Will?*

A. Yes. Attorneys who prepare Trusts usually prepare what is known as a pour-over Will to complement the Trust. The pour-over Will is very much like a regular Will, but it bequeaths items to the Trust that have not been previously registered to the Trust. Items such as automobiles, clothing, furniture, etc. are bequeathed to individual(s) or to the Trust. The purpose of the pour-over Will is to provide for assets which have not been placed in a Trust.

Assets such as real property could be registered to a Trust by deeding the property from John Doe to John Doe, Trustee UTD (under Trust dated) 4/17/85, FBO (for benefit of) John Doe. Stocks, bonds, money market accounts, bank accounts would be registered the same way. All items that have not been registered in this manner would be bequeathed from the pour-over Will to an individual or to the Trust and would have to be probated.

Most people who have a Living Trust prepared have most of their assets registered in their Trust, and if all of their other assets are less than $25,000.00, there is a very fast and inexpensive probate procedure, called Summary Administration. Estate planning techniques and procedures may sound complicated and bothersome but are usually easy to understand once you apply them to your individual situation.

Pour-over Wills generally contain a "Separate Writing" provision which enables the testator to list on a separate piece of paper his personal assets such as jewelry, clothing, furniture, china, etc. that he desires specific individuals to have upon his death. This may be accomplished without mentioning it in his Will. These items can be listed on a piece of paper, signed by the testator, and attached to the Will. As the items are given away, sold, etc. (before the testator dies), the list can be changed without the aid of an attorney.

The pour-over Will also names a personal representative and successor who is usually the same person as the successor Trustee of the Living Trust (if qualified). In most cases it also has a provision which calls for the waiver of posting bond. Pour-over Wills should be notarized in order that witnesses do not have to be proven.

LOST OR DESTROYED WILLS

Q. *What happens after death if a Will is lost or destroyed?*

A. A Will that has been lost or destroyed can be "re-established" through a court proceeding. A petition must be presented and filed which gives a statement of facts constituting the grounds for which relief is sought. It must also give a statement of the contents of the Will and, if available, a copy of the executed Will as an exhibit. A copy of the executed Will kept in the attorney's office file would be sufficient as an exhibit of a lost Will.

The testimony of each witness in the proceeding must be reduced to writing and filed with the court. If the evidence is sufficient to prove that a Will was in existence and that it was a valid Will, the order from the court would recite the full terms of the Will.

One of the difficulties of a lost or destroyed Will is the presumption that the Will was destroyed or revoked intentionally. Of course, if a Will has been destroyed or revoked purposefully and no other Will can be produced, the testator's estate could pass intestate.

In some cases where a Will was destroyed but the person who destroyed it had become incompetent, the original Will may be proven as it was the testator's true intention of how the estate should pass. It should be noted that only slight competency is required to make a Will and if testimony can be presented that the person signing a Will was knowledgeable to what he was doing and had full understanding of his acts, the Will would probably be held to be valid.

In many cases where the Will is lost or destroyed the proceeding will turn into an "adverse proceeding." In such a case one side will be trying to establish or re-establish the fact that a proper Will existed and was not intentionally destroyed, and the other side will try to prove that since the original Will cannot be found that the testator intentionally destroyed the Will because it was not the desire of the testator to "use" the old Will. Such proceedings are decided upon the facts presented to the court just as any other trial matter.

In matters where Trusts were used in the estate plan and the Trusts have been lost or destroyed, the matter could be decided in civil court rather than probate court and copies of the Trusts may be obtained by anyone who had kept a copy during the "registration of assets" to the Trust.

WILLS—UNDUE INFLUENCE

Q. *Can a Will be overturned for undue influence?*

A. Yes. The free use and exercise of being of sound mind is vitally important and absolutely essential in the validity of a Will. A Will can be void, in whole or in part, if the execution is caused by fraud, duress, menace, undue influence or mistake. Undue influence is a recognized ground for contesting the probate or setting aside a probated Will.

If one is to prove undue influence as required for the invalidation of a Will, that person must prove overpersuasion, duress, force, coercion or artful or fraudulent contrivances to such a degree that the one preparing the Will lost his freedom of thought in preparing and making the final provisions of his Will.

Through the practice of persuasion, pressure, artful or fraudulant contrivances, the Will was prepared subject to the desires and wishes of an overpowering person and not truly in the best wishes or desires of the person preparing the Will.

In order to defeat a Will, undue influence relied on as a ground of contest must have operated on the testator at the time the Will was executed.

KINSHIP AND PERSONAL RELATIONSHIPS

Influence that arises from mere affection, attachment, desire to please or gratify is probably not enough to invalidate a Will. Even if affection which was based on an illogical infatuation is proven, it is probably not enough to prove undue influence.

KINDNESS

Kindness, of itself, does not constitute undue influence nor is it evidence of it. Kind offers and good deeds are not improper and a Will cannot be overturned because such influences produced bequeaths in a Will.

MARITAL RELATIONSHIPS

There is no such thing as a confidential relationship between husband and wife governing contests of Wills. It is possible under special conditions for the wife or husband to exert undue influence in a Will if the emotional, physical or mental condition is impaired.

BENEFICIARY'S HELP IN DRAFTING WILL

Generally, the court views beneficiaries helping draft Wills with disfavor and such circumstances are considered suspicious, inviting close scrutiny.

TESTAMENTARY CAPACITY vs. UNDUE INFLUENCE

If a Will is attacked on the grounds of undue influence, then it has been accepted that the party was of sound mind.

If it can be proven that a Will was executed while one was intoxicated, then the area of competency could be challenged.

UNNATURAL, UNREASONABLE OR UNFAIR CHARACTER OF WILL

The circumstances surrounding a Will that is unnatural, unreasonable, unfair or unjust, is generally regarded as evidence that the issue of fraud or undue influence is present.

DEGREE OF PROOF

Proof of undue influence is difficult and, of course, has to overcome the presumption that the Will expresses the voluntary intent of the testator.

For questions in this area of the law, please seek the advice of a competent attorney specializing in estate planning.

CODICILS

Q. *Please explain what a codicil is and what it can and cannot accomplish.*

A. A codicil is a testamentary document that can effectively add to, alter, delete, revoke or republish a Will. Just as much care and consideration should be given to codicils as the original Will.

The codicil is most often used to refer to an addition to the Will, a change in beneficiaries, or a change in the personal representative. The attorney preparing the codicil will generally have to review the existing Will in order to do a proper job in preparing a codicil.

A list of the items usually included in a codicil are as follows:

- Name and residence (or city/county) of Testator;
- Acknowledgment and identification of the existing Will and existing codicils, if any;
- Acknowledgment of codicil as "first" codicil, "second" codicil, etc.;
- Identification of page, paragraph, or line(s) in Will that need to be changed;
- Specification or description of the modification of Will or prior codicils, if any;
- Acknowledgment of revocation of prior codicils, if any;
- Signature of Testator;
- Proper witnessing;
- Notary (for self-proving Wills).

Codicils, of course, have the same general requirements of a Will in that they must be in writing, properly witnessed, and the testator of sound mind, capable of understanding the instrument he executed.

A common practice for those persons that have lived in another state is to have a codicil prepared, thereby republishing their existing Will and changing their legal residence to Florida and having the codicil notarized (self-proving) so that out-of-state witnesses need not be involved in proving the Will. For many persons, the cost of a simple Will *may* only be $25 to $35 and a codicil may cost that much. Therefore, it may be wise to have a new Will prepared instead of having a codicil prepared.

For those persons that have had "Living Trusts" prepared, the codicil is called an amendment and the same general requirements exist for the name and address of Trustee, acknowledgment of existing documents and expressing the exact changes to be made in the Trust instrument, as well as the other requirements listed above.

Codicils and amendments should not be attempted by those who are not licensed attorneys. Changes on Wills or Trusts, themselves, may make the documents void or voidable and improperly drawn changes may cause confusion as to the Testator's or Trustee's intentions.

DO-IT-YOURSELF PROBLEMS

Q. *What problems could I expect if I prepared my own Will or Trust?*

A. I couldn't possibly try to outline all of the problems one could have, but I will address some of the more common problems or steps.

WITHOUT BOND CLAUSE
A clause in a Will included so that the personal representative may serve without bond or security with full power to do all acts including the sale of real or personal property without court orders. Without this clause the administrative costs will be unnecessarily high.

PERSONAL REPRESENTATIVES
Personal Representatives must be of age, must be a resident of Florida *or* must be direct-line blood descendant or otherwise related as required by law. If an invalid personal representative is named, the court will appoint a personal representative or invalidate the Will.

HONEST ERRORS
Attorneys generally add a clause that states that the personal representative shall not be liable for damages or loss caused by honest errors of judgment

made in any good faith exercise of the discretions given to the personal representative.

WITNESSING

If the Will is not witnessed by two persons who actually saw the Testator sign and saw each other sign, the Will could be invalid.

NOTARIZATION

If the Will is notarized, the notary should not be one of the two witnesses. If the notary properly executes the Will, the witnesses do not have to be "proved" at the time of probate, i.e. the witnesses do not have to appear at the courthouse to sign an affidavit concerning their signature.

TRUST PROBLEMS

The mechanical, administrative problems that are normally associated with the probating of a Will and the compliance with court orders are absent with a Living Trust. The Living Trust is never probated thus many of the problems are eliminated. Living Trust should be witnessed and they should have provisions in some cases that limit the liability of successor Trustees.

The most common problem that persons have following the do-it-yourself "Trust Books" are the requirements of the actual re-registration of the assets to the Trust. There are also pitfalls in the re-registration of real property to a Trust for a "do-it-yourselfer", and the lack of knowledge of what to do with personal items.

It should be obvious that the "do-it-yourselfers" are likely to make mistakes or costly omissions. You should be encouraged to seek an attorney to take care of your estate needs.

REFUSING INHERITANCE

Q. *Can I refuse to accept an inheritance and if so, what procedures should I follow?*

A. Yes, you can refuse to accept an inheritance. Although this is not a commonplace occurrence, it is done and it is possible. Perhaps the most common reason for refusing an inheritance is that accepting additional money would elevate one's status to an unavoidable taxable situation.

The new tax laws make it possible, with careful planning, for a husband *and* wife to leave 1.2 million dollars tax free.

Another fairly common reason for refusing an inheritance is that parents may wish for their children to receive money, rather than receive it themselves. This is more common in older parents who do not need additional income and have left everything to their children anyway. Senior citizens also refuse inheritances in order to avoid receiving additional income which would be taxable.

Property held jointly in an estate may not be refused or "disclaimed" and does not fall under the rules of estate "disclaimers."

Refusing inheritances or estate "disclaimers" can be for all or fractional percentages of properties that one is due to inherit.

A "qualified disclaimer" means an unqualified and permanent refusal to accept an interest in property and must meet four conditions:

- The refusal to accept the property must be in writing;
- The written refusal must be received by the Personal Representative or administrator of the estate not later than nine months after the decedent's death.
- The refusal must be absolute and the property must have never been accepted.
- The person making the refusal cannot direct the redistribution or transfer of the property to another person.

Generally speaking, one method of handling a refusal of inheritance is to bypass the person who is refusing the inheritance as though that person had predeceased the decedent. For example, if the Will states 50% to my brother, John, and if he is not living, then to his children . . . If John makes a "qualified disclaimer," then his children could receive the estate.

Refusals or disclaimers can be used very effectively in tax planning and altering the distribution under a Will.

As with all financial planning, seek the assistance of a qualified attorney.

INTESTATE WITHOUT SPOUSE

Q. *What would happen to an estate if a person died without a Will and without a spouse?*

A. Florida Statutes have made your Will for you if you choose not to make one yourself. If you die without a spouse, your estate would pass as follows:

1. To the lineal descendants of the deceased.
2. If there are no lineal descendants, to the descendant's father and mother equally, or to the survivor of them.
3. If there are no lineal descendants and the decedent's father and mother have predeceased, then to the brothers and sisters of the decedent and descendants of brothers and sisters.

4. If none of the above exist, then the estate shall be divided one-half to the decedent's paternal kindred and one-half to the decedent's maternal kindred in the following fashion:

    (a) To the grandfather and grandmother in equal shares or to the survivor if one is deceased.

    (b) If the grandmother and grandfather have predeceased, then to the uncles and aunts and descendants of the deceased, then to the uncles and aunts and descendants of the deceased uncles and aunts of the decedent.

    (c) If there are no paternal or maternal kindred, the estate shall pass as follows: To the kindred of the last deceased spouse of the decedent as if the deceased spouse had survived the decedent and then died intestate entitled to the estate.

The Florida Statutes also have rules regarding adopted persons and how they are included in distribution of an estate where there is no Will. The adopted person is considered a lineal descendant of the adopting parent and is one of the natural kindred of all members of the adopting parent's family, and he/she is not a lineal descendant of his/her natural parents and is not part of the kindred of the natural family.

A person born out of wedlock is considered a lineal descendant of his/her mother and is one of the natural kindred of all members of the mother's family. The person born out of wedlock could be a lineal descendant and part of the natural kindred of the father's family if the parents marry before or after the birth or if the father is established by a court order.

Of course, all proceedings regarding the above would be under the supervision of the probate court and subject to higher than normal probate fees. Careful planning of your estate can reduce and sometimes eliminate probate, and your Will or Trust will eliminate confusion as to who your beneficiaries are.

LIFE ESTATES

Q. *In my Will I am considering bequeathing my house to my sister for life and upon her death to my children. What are the disadvantages of such an arrangement?*

A. There are many advantages as well as disadvantages in establishing a life estate. The first advantage is that your sister will never own the property and she cannot disregard the rights of your children (called remaindermen). The children, however, have very little opportunity to take an active part in the ownership, if any, and often find themselves powerless.

A life tenant, generally, is not subject to supervision by any court or even accountable to any court unless some action is brought against him. If an action against a life tenant is presented to the court and allegations of undue waste or encroachment are found, then a court may issue an order to protect against undue waste or encroachment. Often if a life tenant has a "power to consume" there is very little a remainderman can do to protect his rights.

A life tenant is normally required to pay taxes upon the property of the tenancy and also to pay interest on a mortgage that existed at the time of the creation of the life estate, but is entitled to contribution from remaindermen for payment of the debt secured by the mortgage.

The powers of a life tenant are determined by the terms of the gift. In most cases, there is not a power of sale, however, a life tenant may be able to sell his life estate under some circumstances.

An alternative to leaving a life estate in a Will is setting up a life estate through a "Living Trust" and after death, having a successor Trustee manage a life estate for a third party with distribution of the estate upon the death of the life tenant. In this manner the life tenant never actually has possession because the successor Trustee controls the property. The life tenant still, of course, has use of the property.

DISINHERITING CHILDREN?

Q. *Can a parent disinherit a child?*

A. Yes, a parent may disinherit his or her child as well as any illegitimate child. This may be accomplished by omitting the child from the Will. The most common way to do this is to mention the child's name in the Will but to leave him a nominal sum of money and to perhaps make some statement concerning him.

The Florida Statutes refer to "pretermission*" which means "permitted" or omitted from the Will of the testator. Most states have pretermission statutes which usually provide that a "pretermitted heir" takes the same share of the estate which he would have received if the testator had died intestate (without a Will), unless the omission was intentional and not due to mistake or accident. The main purpose of pretermission statutes is to avoid an unintentional or inadvertent disinheritance of a child.

As long as they are minors, legitimate and illegitimate children *may* have certain rights to support even if they are omitted from a Will. This support may be obtained through the probate courts under the "Family Allowance" statutes. In addition, social security benefits may be available, and in some cases recovery for wrongful death may be obtained.

INHERITANCE AND MURDER

Q. *Can a person convicted of murder still be entitled to receive an inheritance?*

A. No. A person convicted of the murder of a decedent is not entitled to inherit from the decedent or take any part of the estate as a devisee. The part of the decedent's estate which the murderer would have received would pass to the persons entitled to it as though the murderer had died during the lifetime of the decedent. For example:

> To murderer, and if he is not living, then to his wife and children. (If murderer is convicted, the estate would pass to his family.)
>
> or
>
> To murderer, and if he is not living, his share shall lapse. (The estate would be left to the other beneficiaries named in the Will or Trust.)

It would appear from Florida case law that a murderer who is acquitted on grounds of insanity could still receive a distribution from the estate of the decedent. One case found that an insane wife who killed her husband was still entitled to her statutory share of the estate and another case stated that an insane son could inherit part of an estate from his father.

In another case a widow was acquitted for murdering her husband due to insanity, but she was not allowed to collect from the insurance company as primary beneficiary because one cannot profit from his own wrong.

In cases where property is held as tenants by the entirety, and the husband murdered his wife and then he committed suicide, it has been generally held that the heirs of each (assuming no children) would each receive one-half of the estate.

In all cases it can be said that one murdering his ancestors should be required to forfeit his right of inheritance, and his guilt should be established beyond a reasonable doubt. In addition to not being entitled to receive any inheritance, it should also be stated that a convicted murderer would not be entitled to be appointed as personal representative of an estate.

IN TERROREM CLAUSE

Q. *Can I omit all of my heirs from receiving anything at my death?*

A. In previous pages we have addressed the rights that a spouse may have absent a prenuptial agreement, therefore that subject will not be covered in this writing.

You may generally omit heirs other than a wife. Some of the most common pitfalls which are used by heirs to contest a Will are as follows:

1. Deceased made a mistake by forgetting to mention heir in the Will;
2. Deceased was incompetent when Will was made;
3. Deceased was under "undue influence" when Will was made.

It is usually sufficient to state in a Will that you have omitted (. . . my son, ADAM, of my first marriage, for personal reasons.) Some attorneys take this one step further and state:

> "In the event that my son or any heir or person claiming to be an heir shall contest in any court any of the provisions of this instrument, or who shall not defend or assist in good faith in the defense of any or all such contests, then each and all such persons shall not be entitled to any devises, legacies or benefits under this Will or Codicil thereto, and to each of such persons I hereby bequeath the sum of One Dollar ($1.00) only."

This clause should be recognized as an "in terrorem" clause and is never 100% safe from attack. However, it is the suggestion by the writer that, at a minimum, those you wish to disinherit should be mentioned in your Will and stated that they are omitted.

Some attorneys use what is known as a "savings clause" which states that if any part, clause, provision, or condition of the Will should be held to be void, invalid or inoperative, that the invalidity shall not affect any other clause, provision, or condition of the remainder of the Will.

It should be noted that it is much more effective to omit individuals by name rather than to state, "I omit all other individuals not mentioned in this Will." Courts will generally uphold the desires of individuals when specific identification has been made. The small omission clause that may be placed in a Will (regular or pour-over) may also be placed in a Living Trust.

The use of video in Wills is becoming popular which enables the testator to explain on video the reason he has omitted persons in his Will or Trust.

PER STIRPES OR PER CAPITA

Q. *What is the difference between per stirpes and per capita?*

A. One of the most often asked questions is what does per stirpes or per capita mean. Per stirpes means "according to the roots, or by right of representation." The issue of deceased children will take their deceased parent's share by right of representation. For example, suppose a decedent had three children, X, Y, and Z. The decedent's Will stated that X, Y, and Z would receive the estate in three equal shares, and if X, Y, or Z had predeceased, then his/her share would pass to his/her children, per stirpes. If Z predeceased the decedent, then Z's share (or 1/3 of the estate) would be distributed equally to his children. The distribution would be 1/3 to X, 1/3 to Y, and 1/3 to the children of Z.

If the Will had stated to X, Y, and Z, and if not living, then to their children, per capita, the estate would be divided as follows: Suppose X had no children, Y had no children, and Z had ten children. If Z had predeceased, then the estate would be divided between X, Y, and ten children in equal shares, in other words 12 equal shares. Per capita means equally or share and share alike.

A common clause using per capita would be "should any beneficiary predeceased me leaving children surviving me, such children shall take per capita, share and share alike, and not per stirpes." A common per stirpes clause would be, "one-third (1/3) to X, and if he is not living, then to his lineal descendants, per stirpes, and not per capita."

As you can see, the words per stirpes and per capita can make a tremendous difference in the amount of money a beneficiary would receive. Before one chooses the method of distribution, he should fully understand the consequences of his decision. The use of the words, per stirpes and per capita, can be used in either a Will or a Living Trust as they are commonly known terms in estate planning. Generally speaking, a greater number of people plan their estates "per stirpes" rather than "per capita," leaving family units equal shares rather than individuals.

CONVENIENCE AND JOINT ACCOUNTS

Q. *My mother's Will is being contested due to a dispute over a convenience account. What is the difference between a convenience account and a joint account?*

A. A convenience account is a deposit account other than a certificate of deposit, in the name of one individual (principal), in which one or more other individuals have signing authority on the account. The designation of other persons having authority on the account can only be made by the principal. Generally, it can be stated that it is *not* affected by the subsequent death or incompetence of the principal.

The principal, however, is the only one who has all of the rights, interest and claims to the deposits and monies in said account. Banks may release monies to appointed guardians and personal representatives of the principal without regard to any agents the personal representative may have appointed.

Joint accounts are accounts set up in names of two or more persons. It is presumed that the survivor shall have all rights, title, interest and claim to such accounts. The presumption can be overturned by proof of fraud or undue influence or clear and convincing proof of a contrary intent. It should be noted that joint accounts are stronger than a Will and the distribution clause in a Will has no effect on accounts that have been established jointly.

For a joint account to be deemed a "convenience account" there would have to be clear and convincing evidence that the account was for the benefit of the principal.

Bank accounts established "in Trust for" are generally presumed to be created for (upon death) the benefit of the person designated on the account.

Many persons fall into the trap of setting up several accounts as described above and having a Will which leaves everything "equally to the children." The problem is that everything would be left equally to the children *except* the joint or "in Trust for" accounts. Those accounts would pass to the survivor or the person designated "in Trust for." Convenience accounts may be cashed out without the other beneficiaries' knowledge.

Planning your estate will require a thorough analysis of your assets and help from your attorney.

NECESSITY OF WILLS

Q. *Is it true that you don't need a Will if:*
1. *You don't have enough assets to bother;*
2. *You are single;*
3. *Your spouse will automatically get everything;*
4. *All of your assets are owned jointly with right of survivorship.*

A. All four assumptions could easily be wrong.
1. Any size estate is large enough to have a Will, and if you take the time to compile a list of assets, you will probably be surprised at the size of your estate. Your estate also includes the proceeds from life insurance, your home, car, antiques, etc. Failure to have a Will prepared will also mean that whatever assets you do have will be distributed according to state statutes instead of your personal choice.
2. Being single is no excuse for not preparing a Will. If you fail to prepare a Will, you have failed to choose to whom your assets will be distributed. Simple Wills are not costly and should be prepared to assure your assets will pass exactly where you desire upon your death. Single persons should also consider a durable family power of attorney and/or a Living Trust to plan for possible accidents, strokes, or senility.
3. The surviving spouse does not automatically receive everything in the absence of a Will in Florida. When you die without a Will, your spouse only receives part of the estate with the other part going to the deceased person's children. Failure to have a Will also means failure to appoint a guardian for minor children, which generally leads to unnecessary expenses of the estate.
4. Joint ownership does not necessarily replace the need for Wills. Should a husband and wife be in an accident and both die simultaneously, and both did not have a Will, the entire estate would be distributed under the laws of intestacy (without a Will). Another consideration is if one became incapacitated and the other dies—the entire estate will pass through intestacy.

The basic difference in having a Will and not having one is the difference in being in control or being out of control of your assets. Simple Wills are inexpensive and can be prepared in a very short time (some while you wait). If you visit an attorney you should also discuss the advantages of a Living Trust.

PERSONAL REPRESENTATIVES

PERSONAL REPRESENTATIVES

Q. *What is a Personal Representative? Please outline the duties of a Personal Representative when a Testator dies.*

A. A Personal Representative is one who will settle and administer your estate upon your death. He has a very important function and usually works very closely with an attorney to probate the estate. Much care and consideration should be given when appointing or selecting a Personal Representative to your Will. There are as many as 60 or 70 separate duties and tasks that a Personal Representative could be required to perform. He normally collects and takes inventory assets, determines debts and claims against one's estate, manages the estate during the settlement and files appropriate income tax forms. He can, while working along with an attorney, distribute the assets to the beneficiaries of the estate. There are many duties of which I will summarize and outline that a Personal Representative could become involved in.

The first phase of activity that the Personal Representative will be involved in will be locating assets and collecting information. Examples of this would be (1) to locate the Will and have it filed; (2) examine inventory of the safety deposit box; (3) obtain the death certificate; (4) collect all information regarding insurance; (4) collect all bills, i.e. doctor bills, etc. involving the person's estate; (5) check out burial instructions; (6) work with the Internal Revenue Service or the Social Security Administration regarding payments and outstanding checks; (7) list and locate inventory bank accounts; (8) collect and assemble all stocks and bonds; (9) locate named beneficiaries and next of kin; (10) collect and inventory deeds and other property owned; (11) investigate the status of any stocks or business ownership the person may be involved in; and finally (12) inventory such personal items as jewelry, furniture and automobiles.

The next phase of the duties of the Personal Representative is determining debts and claims that may be made against the estate. This, of course, will involve collecting information about monies due on charge accounts, mortgages, life insurance, and so on.

The third phase of activity for the Personal Representative is to actually manage the estate. This is accomplished by (1) setting up bookkeeping records; (2) registering stocks and bonds; (3) inventorying all items of property and making arrangements for their distribution; (4) reviewing all investments as to safety and quality; (5) examining books and records of any business interests which may need audits and appraisals; and, upon occasion, supervising and continuing to run the family business.

The fourth phase of activity is to wrap up the decedent's income tax determinations to decide how much tax is due and how that tax should be paid out of which accounts. This involves preparing the estate's final income tax return. Upon occasion, money will have to be raised or items will have to be sold in order to pay the last tax before any distribution could be made. The payment of personal property and real estate taxes should also be taken care of in this phase.

27

The final phase in which the Personal Representative must be involved is to distribute the assets within the estate. This phase involves determining who is entitled to what and how that beneficiary will receive what he is entitled to. Often assets have to be sold to take care of specific cash distributions called for in the Last Will & Testament or Trust. During this phase all the final costs of the estate must be paid and often re-registration of securities will have to be accomplished in order to make cash distributions.

A Personal Representative must meet certain qualifications in the State of Florida if he or she is to serve as a Personal Representative. The qualifications of a Personal Representative are set forth in the Florida Statutes. No person can serve as a Personal Representative if under eighteen years of age. A non-resident cannot serve unless such person is a legally adopted child of the decedent or an adopted parent or is related by lineal consanguinity to the decedent, is a spouse, or brother, sister, uncle, aunt, nephew or niece of the decedent or is the spouse of any such person. All Trust companies incorporated under the laws of the State and all national banking associations authorized and qualified to exercise fiduciary powers in Florida are entitled to act as Personal Representatives and curators of estates.

Unless waived by a Will, an individual serving as a Personal Representative is required to give bond, as required by Florida Statutes. Even if this requirement is waived by the Will, most courts insist that a person living outside of the county will be required to be bonded.

Very often a person will make a loved one or family member a Personal Representative. This may not always be the best policy. For example, if a loved one is made a Personal Representative and the loved one has absolutely no financial experience, the results can often be nightmarish. Much care and thought should be given to the selection of a Personal Representative. The person must be financially astute and capable of understanding exactly what is needed to be an effective Personal Representative. The person must be totally capable of managing their own affairs and perhaps the success in which that person has in that area should be used to measure the success in taking care of someone else's affairs.

If no family member is considered to be capable of being the Personal Representative, the Testator should consider the use of a professional person such as an attorney or accountant or use the professional service of a financial institution such as a bank that has a Trust department. Often this type individual or institution has the experience that is needed to carefully manage same. This may be particularly important if there is a business that is an ongoing concern and needs to be managed while within the estate. This type of Personal Representative needs to be unbiased and objective yet sympathetic to the needs of the family during the administration of the estate.

A Personal Representative is entitled to a reasonable fee for his services during the administration and probate of the estate. No flat or fixed fee is used in the State of Florida, but fees may be obtained by strictly submitting expenses and a bill for the reasonable amount of time that the Personal Representative has spent on the estate. In addition to the Personal Representative's fee, the attorney will charge a probate fee for administering the estate. Very often there will be two fees, i.e. the Personal Representative's fee and the attorney's fee, which will be subtracted from the total estate.

REMOVAL OF PERSONAL REPRESENTATIVE

Q. *Can a Personal Representative be removed from an estate?*

A. Yes. The court may remove a Personal Representative from an estate. The court has broad powers to protect estates and Florida Statute 733.504 also lists causes for which a personal representative may be removed. Some of the reasons for removal are:

1. A determination of incompetency, or even if not a determination or adjudication, any cause or reason, mental or physical which renders the Personal Representative incapable of discharging his duties.
2. Refusal or failure to comply with an order of the probate court unless the order is superceded or appealed.
3. Refusal or failure to file proper accountings, obtain proper orders for the sale of items, or produce items for inspection.
4. Wasting, self-profiteering, mismanagement or maladministration of the estate.
5. Failure to post bond or give security (if required by the court).
6. The insolvency or bankruptcy of a corporate Personal Representative or upon the conviction of a felony by an individual Personal Representative.
7. Conflict of interest or adverse interests against an estate where self-interest may be more important than the interest of the estate. Surviving spouses named as Personal Representative do not usually have a problem with conflict of interest.
8. The revocation of probate of a Will will cease the Personal Representative's function.
9. A Personal Representative not being domiciled in Florida is grounds for removal.

Generally speaking, most grounds for removal seem to center around mismanagement of the estate such as failure to timely file answers to creditors' claims against the estate. Usually the court has wide discretion on grounds of removal.

Proceedings to remove a Personal Representative may be initiated by any interested person, the Court or a joint Personal Representative. It should be noted that attorneys acting as Personal Representatives can also be removed if needed to protect an estate.

UNNAMED PERSONAL REPRESENTATIVES

Q. *How are Personal Representatives selected when one dies intestate?*

A. First, let's answer the various ways a Personal Representative is selected with a Will (testate). The Personal Representative may be:

1. The person nominated in the Will (if qualified);
2. The person selected by a majority of the interested parties entitled to the estate;
3. A person who is a devisee (beneficiary) who applies to be a Personal Representative. If more than one applies, the court shall select the most qualified.

In estates where a Will was never made (intestate), the Personal Representative may be:

1. The surviving spouse;
2. The person selected by a majority of those with an interest in the estate (heirs);
3. The closest heir or, in the court's discretion, the most qualified heir;
4. A guardian of the property of the ward. If this person does not wish to be appointed he may exercise the right to appoint someone;
5. The court may appoint someone who is qualified to act as Personal Representative.

The person selected may not hold public office, or be employed by the court, or work for any judge. He will not be qualified if he has been convicted of a felony, or if he is physically unable to perform the duties, or is under the age of 18 years.

A nonresident of Florida cannot qualify as Personal Representative unless he is:

1. Related by lineal consanguinity to the decedent;
2. Legally adopted child or adoptive parent of the decedent;
3. A spouse, brother, sister, uncle, aunt, nephew, or niece of the decedent;
4. A spouse of a person otherwise qualified as above.

If a Will names a person who is not qualified in Florida, the next person named as Successor Personal Representative would qualify to serve. If no one named qualifies, the court will appoint someone as mentioned previously.

Selecting a Personal Representative is a big decision in planning one's estate. The individual should be competent, trustworthy, available, and have the necessary time to spend with the attorney as the estate goes through probate. Personal Representatives are entitled to a reasonable fee for their services.

The rigid requirements of who may be a Personal Representative are not present when selecting a Trustee of a Living Trust.

PROBATE

COST OF PROBATE

Q. *What does it cost to probate an estate?*

A. This question is much too broad to give a precise answer. The word "estate" means many things to many people. There is an old saying, "what you don't know about probate costs is enough to kill you."

Probate attorneys work in many different ways, with some charging a fee per hour, some charging a flat fee, and some charging a percentage of the estate, or possibly a combination of all of the above.

Based on a table from "Federal Estate and Gift Tax Reports" published by the Commerce Clearing House, the estimated probate and administrative costs of an estate are as follows:

Cost of Probate

Estate $10,000	Cost $850
Estate $20,000	Cost $1,700
Estate $50,000	Cost $4,300
Estate $100,000	Cost $7,900
Estate $150,000	Cost $11,200
Estate $200,000	Cost $14,400
Estate $260,000	Cost $18,100
Estate $380,000	Cost $24,900
Estate $500,000	Cost $35,000
Estate $700,000	Cost $46,900
Estate 1,000,000	Cost $64,000
Estate 10,000,000	Cost $520,000

These figures should be considered as "possible costs" and as was explained above, different attorneys have different methods of charging.

Attorneys who prepare Wills and hold on to the original of that Will do not have to be the same one who probates the Will. The beneficiaries should be able to choose any attorney they desire, and inquiring as to attorney fees from several different attorneys would be appropriate.

There are many steps that can be taken to avoid probate. One of the most popular methods is to have a Living Trust.

The principal advantages of a Trust are:

(a) Avoids probate costs
(b) Immediate distribution of assets as opposed to 6 or 12 months or longer with a Will
(c) Private (not a matter for public records)
(d) Avoids some guardianship problems

SMALL ESTATE ADMINISTRATION

Q. *Is there a simple probate procedure for small estates?*

A. Yes. There is a procedure for estates that do not exceed $25,000. The procedure is called "Summary Administration" and is a much faster procedure than "Formal Administration." Generally speaking, the requirements in the petition and information needed are set forth below.

- Petitioner needs to state what interest he/she has in the estate. For example, the Petitioner may be the Personal Representative of the deceased's Will. There may be more than one Petitioner and their addresses and the name and address of their attorney are also required.

- Information concerning the decedent including last address, age, Social Security number, date of death and domicile (county residing) is also necessary.

- The names, addresses, relationship and ages of the beneficiaries must also be included in the Petition. If one of the beneficiaries is a minor, the birth date must be included.

- The Petitioner must state why the Petition is being filed in that particular county. In other words, the court needs to decide if proper venue has been established.

- The assets of the deceased must be listed in the Petition along with the estimated value of same as well as those assets that are claimed to be exempt. The inventory list must be reasonably accurate and complete.

- The Petitioner must make a statement that the assets do not exceed $25,000.

- A list of creditors, their addresses and amount of debt should also be included in the Petition. If payments of the debt have been arranged, the arrangements should be specified in the Petition.

- The Petitioner should also state that he/she is unaware of any other Will or unrevoked Codicil of the decedent.

- The original Will must have been previously filed with the court (and so stated) or must accompany the Petition.

- The Will, itself, must not have directed formal administration under the Florida Statutes.

- A proposed plan of distribution of the assets is set forth in the Petition and an Order of Summary Administration is asked for.

Summary Administration can be a very useful tool for those who have a large majority of their assets in a revocable Living Trust and less than $25,000 of their assets are left in a "Pour-Over" Will.

EXEMPT PROPERTY & FAMILY ALLOWANCE

Q. *What property can pass to a spouse upon death as "exempt property" and what property can pass under "family allowance?"*

A. Homestead property passes to the spouse along with certain exempt property if the surviving spouse was domiciled in Florida at the time of the other spouse's death, subject to any perfected security interest, to household furniture, furnishings, and appliances in the decedent's usual place of abode, up to $10,000 and the surviving spouse is entitled, subject to any perfected security interest, to all automobiles held in the decedent's name.

The surviving spouse is also entitled to, as exempt property, personal effects up to a value of $1,000 unless the personal effects are disposed of by Will or Trust. These exempt properties are in addition to any benefit or share passing to the surviving spouse or minor children by the Will of the decedent.

In addition to the homestead and exempt property, if the decedent was domiciled in Florida at the time of death, the surviving spouse and the deceased's lineal heirs whom he was obligated to support, are entitled to a reasonable allowance in money for their maintenance while the estate is in probate. After notice and hearing, the court may order this allowance to be paid in lump sum or in periodic installments. This allowance may not exceed $6,000. If the spouse dies shortly thereafter or has already predeceased, then the guardian or one taking care of the children, providing for their care and custody, would be entitled to receive payments. Family allowance is generally for those in an emergency situation for a family in need of funds.

A Homestead may not be subject to devise if the owner is survived by a spouse or minor children, except the homestead may be given to a spouse if there are no children. Of course, the homestead which is owned jointly by husband and wife, and one dies, the surviving spouse becomes the owner.

Homestead, exempt property, and family allowance take preference over the bequests in a Will.

FAMILY ADMINISTRATION

Q. *What is Family Administration (Probate)?*

A. Family Administration is a way to probate an estate under simplified rules and procedures within a shorter period of time than it would take for normal probate. Family administration is available when it appears:

1. The heirs at law of the decedent are a surviving spouse and/or lineal descendants, and the decedent did not leave a Will;

2. The decedent left a Will and the beneficiaries are the surviving spouse and/or lineal descendants, and they are the major benefactors of the estate;
3. The Will does not direct probate under the Rules of Chapter 733 under the Probate Code;
4. The value of the gross estate for federal tax purposes is less than $60,000.00;
5. The claims of creditors have been generally processed or barred.

The petition for Family Administration shall be verified by all of the beneficiaries and shall show the facts that the petitioners are entitled to Family Administration. It also shows a complete list of the assets of the gross estate for federal estate tax purposes and a statement that the estate is not indebted, or that provision for payments has been made, or the claims are barred. A schedule of distribution of the assets is also included in the petition.

After the petition is filed the Will is proven in the normal fashion. If the estate consists of personal property only, the court may enter an order for immediate distribution.

Under Family Administration the petitioners are personally liable for all lawful claims against the estate of the decedent but only to the extent of the value of the estate received by the petitioners (unless exempt). Generally, claims may not be made against the estate or the petitioners after three years from the death of the decedent.

If any heir who was lawfully entitled to receive a share of the estate was omitted from the petition and not included in the Order of Family Administration, he may enforce his rights in the appropriate proceedings, and if successful, shall be entitled to attorney's fees.

In summary, Family Administration is a way to settle an estate when the assets are $60,000.00 or less and other criteria as described above are met. It is a shorter procedure than regular probate proceedings.

PROBATING PERSONAL ITEMS

Q. *How do you probate "personal items?"*

A. A search of the residence of the deceased should be made and each item should be counted and included on the "estate" inventory form to be filed with the court. The list should be thorough and particular.

A sample inventory would be as follows:

> *LIVING ROOM*
> Sofa & 2 matching chairs

2 table lamps
3 oil paintings
2 mirrors
1 oriental rug
1 grandfather clock

KITCHEN
G.E. refrigerator
G.E. stove/oven
1 Mr. Coffee
1 kitchen table
4 kitchen chairs
8 place settings of china
8 place settings of silverware
Various pots, pans, utensils

Each room would be inventoried and added to the list of items, including books, tools, and a mention of the clothing. The safe deposit box should also be inventoried and a complete list made including all coins, bonds, stocks, deeds, notes, mortgages and even papers of no apparent value.

This inventory list is filed in the court, made a part of the public records, and made available for anyone to see.

If the entire estate is left to one person a shorter method may be advisable if an appraiser would come to the deceased's residence and place a value on all the items and issue an appraisal report. Nevertheless, a complete list should be made for tax and insurance considerations.

If the personal representative undertakes to perform the inventory, he should be accompanied by a witness to the actual inventory of items.

There are many types of "personal items" and this article could not possibly cover all of them. When you are having your attorney prepare your Will, you should have him explain the "Separate Writing" clause regarding personal effects. A discussion should possibly also take place regarding a "Revocable Living Trust" and the avoidance of the probate procedure.

PROBATING THE AUTOMOBILE

Q. *How do you probate an automobile?*

A. The executor or personal representative of a Will often has trouble deciding what to do with an automobile.

Of utmost concern is the fact that an auto can be an extremely dangerous item and many lawsuits arise from traffic accidents.

If the auto has been left to a member of the family, title of the car should be transferred before the family member takes over and drives it. If an accident occurs, the "estate" and the family member could be liable for damages.

If the car has been left to someone outside the family, the car should be stored, appraised and then transferred. A proper accounting should be made to the court of any and all transactions.

If the car is part of the general estate, it should probably be sold as soon as possible. The Will will probably give the power to sell the car, but if not, a court order can be obtained to sell the vehicle. The executor should obtain proper appraisals, both retail and wholesale.

Once the power to sell the car is established, it can be sold at public or private sale. The ideal sale will have three sealed bids, but this is not always possible. In the care of cars there is usually little criticism involved in quick sales rather than holding out for "top dollar."

If the personal representative is concerned about accepting a low bid, he or she can obtain approval from the beneficiaries or possibly get approval from the court.

One of the most important steps is to make absolutely sure that the car is adequately insured and that liability, collision and comprehensive insurance are properly maintained.

If one has a revocable Living Trust, then a discussion between the Trustees and the attorney should decide if the car should be placed in the Trust.

PROBATING A BUSINESS

Q. *What should I do to protect my business during incapacity or death?*

A. Businesses need to be protected when a key member dies or becomes incompetent. Problems such as who has the authority to continue the business, what the business is worth, and what personnel will manage the business are often vital factors that can make the difference regarding the survival or failure of the business.

If a sole proprietor dies with a Will, his personal representative must act quickly with appropriate court orders to have the business continued. If the business is to continue, then decisions must be made concerning who will run the business, what levels of activity will continue in various areas, what financing will be needed, and who will be kept on the payroll.

In many instances the best plan for a business is that it be sold, with the money therefrom being distributed to the heirs of the deceased. Planning ahead is also very important regarding the sale of a business because of the many ways in which a business can be evaluated. If there are several partners or major stockholders in a business, a buy-sell agreement should be a mandatory item.

Buy-sell agreements, if properly prepared, will avoid the arguments over business evaluation after the death of one of the owners.

If the personal representative of a Will decides to continue the business, he will submit a petition to the court which shall include:

1. A statement of the nature of that business or venture;
2. A schedule of specific assets and liabilities;
3. The reasons for continuation;
4. The proposed form and times of accounting for that business or venture;
5. The period for which the continuation is requested; and
6. Any other information pertinent to the petition.

Many business owners put their business interests in a Trust which appoints a committee to carry on the business upon the death or incapacity of the owner. The Trust also describes in great detail exactly what the committee can and cannot do and what financial and managerial duties are expected. The advantages of a Business Trust is that the committee established in the Trust can operate without court orders and without the business passing through probate. The committee is comprised of exactly the members chosen by the business owner. The committee is often very experienced personnel who are familiar with all of the aspects of running the business. Often the committee will be given the instruction to run the business only until it can be sold.

AVOIDING PROBATE

Q. *How can I avoid the probating of my estate?*

A. First, we should define probate as most people do not understand what it means.

"Probate is the administration of estates." A personal representative or attorney will present your Will (if you have one) to the probate court with an inventory of assets and liabilities of your estate. The procedure of administering or carrying out your last wishes and desires and the expense involved in changing title to property is called probate. Probate as defined in *Black's Law Dictionary* is "the act or process of proving a Will."

Contrary to popular belief, items or property that are left in a Will (unless jointly held) *do* have to be probated. Thus, items left to your children or other family members would have to go through the probate procedure. This procedure could easily take up to one year or more and be of considerable expense. Those persons who die without a Will leave their estate exposed to the State of Florida in providing a Will and deciding upon the personal representative.

AVOIDING PROBATE

There are three kinds of property which can pass to your heirs at your death without going through the probate procedure. They are:

1. Most property owned jointly with the right of survivorship;
2. Property held in a Living Trust;
3. Life insurance payable to a named beneficiary.

It should be pointed out that not all property held jointly avoids probate; that Trusts created in Wills do not avoid probate; and that insurance held to the estate does not avoid probate.

Careful estate planning often involves the teamwork of an attorney, a CPA or accountant, an insurance agent and a financial planner. Of all the above mentioned, the attorney should control the input from the other team members and only he is authorized to practice law and advise you of the legal ramifications of your estate plan.

You should be extremely cautious of persons offering to provide estate analysis who are merely trying to sell you a product. Such decisions should be reviewed with an attorney.

Avoiding probate does not automatically provide for the avoidance of unnecessary taxes. Improper estate planning can leave many tax surprises which can be avoided. Full advantage should be taken of the new tax laws which allow the passing of $600,000.00 tax free (estates) in 1987, and the $10,000.00 gift tax rule.

There are also many tax considerations in charitable giving, including:

1. Annuity Trust;
2. The Unitrust;
3. The Pooled income fund.

Competent counsel can assist you in properly planning your estate and devising a plan offering you enjoyment of income, preserving your estate for your loved ones, and taking full advantage of all possible tax considerations.

GUARDIANSHIP

GUARDIANSHIPS

Q. *What are the different types of guardianships in Florida?*

A. Florida statutes define several different types of guardianships:

1. GUARDIAN OF THE PERSON:
   Guardians of the Person are charged with the ward's personal care. If the guardianship is of a minor, then education and training of the ward are provided for. If the ward is physically or mentally incompetent, then a guardian of the person must be appointed. Also, if the ward in incompetent, then an annual examination of the ward must take place with the results being reported to the court. Generally speaking, guardians of adults provide for them a style of living to which they are accustomed, if it is economically feasible.

2. GUARDIAN OF PROPERTY:
   Guardians appointed by the court either because of incompetency or for a minor, take possession and control of the ward's property assets and income. The guardian is generally charged with handling the ward's property under the "reasonable man or prudent man" rule. If the guardian has special skills, then the standards of care are higher and he must exercise whatever skills he has in the management of the ward's assets.

3. NATURAL GUARDIANS:
   Florida statutes define "natural guardians" as the parents of minor children. Upon death, natural guardianship would pass to the surviving parent and upon divorce, the guardian would be the one given custody of the child. The mother is most often considered the natural guardian of a child born out of wedlock.

4. TESTAMENTARY GUARDIAN:
   Florida statutes authorize parents to name a guardian for minor children in a Will. Guardians so named are subject to Florida law, just as any other guardian would be. The court system does not usually involve itself with guardians named by Will unless charges or allegations are made concerning the fitness or capability of a guardian.

5. VOLUNTARY GUARDIANSHIP:
   A resident or nonresident may petition the court for a "voluntary guardianship" without an adjudication of incompetency. The petition must include a physician's statement that the petitioner understands the nature of his acts and requests. Guardians of this type have the same responsibilities as other guardians.

6. CONSERVATORS:
   If a person can be established as a "missing person" under Florida statutes, a conservator under certain circumstances may be appointed. Conservators have the same responsibilities, rights and duties as guardians of property.

INCOMPETENCY AND GUARDIANSHIP

Q. *Could you please explain how one obtains the status of incompetent and how a guardian is appointed?*

A. If one is suspected, with reasonable proof, of being incompetent by reason of mental illness, sickness, excessive use of alcohol or drugs, or other mental or physical condition so that he is incapable of caring for himself or managing his property or is likely to dissipate or lose his property or inflict harm upon himself or upon others, the State may hold "inquisition proceedings."

These proceedings are always held in the circuit court of the jurisdiction where the alleged incompetent resides. The only issue to be decided in these proceedings is to decide the status of the alleged incompetent. Every alleged incompetent must be afforded an opportunity to be represented by counsel and if unable to afford counsel one will be appointed by the court.

The petition may be filed by:

1. Father, mother, brother, sister, spouse, adult child, next of kin;
2. Any three citizens of the State;
3. A person who requests the examination himself (certificate from a Florida doctor);
4. Medical director of a state correctional institution concerning a person at the institution.

Trial by jury is not applicable in situations of this nature. The judge will normally appoint two practicing physicians, who may not be associated in practice and are responsible citizens, to form a committee. This committee will issue a report as to the mental or physical competency of the alleged incompetent to the court.

If the alleged incompetent is found physically or mentally incompetent the court will appoint a personal guardian, and a guardian of the property may also be appointed. If the person is found competent, the petition will be dropped.

After a judgment adjudicating a person to be mentally or physically incompetent is filed, he is presumed for the duration of the incompetency incapable of managing his own affairs and also incapable of making gifts, contracts or any instruments binding on an estate. The filing of the judgment constitutes notice of the incompetency.

If one is adjudicated incompetent, the right of appeal is always available. If one is hospitalized, a certificate of competency is issued when the person is capable of managing his own affairs.

Quite often a husband or wife becomes a guardian by court order by the above proceedings to manage the other half of the joint estate. The proceedings are always open to the public and made part of the court record.

GUARDIANSHIP DUTIES

Q. *I am concerned that I may have to be appointed Guardian for my mother. What duties and responsibilities will I have to the court?*

A. Some of the duties and responsibilities of Guardians are:

- *Bond*—Guardians' bond must be in an amount equal to the full amount of cash on hand plus the value of note, bonds or any other negotiable assets of the *ward* (a child or incompetent person placed by law under the care of a guardian or court).

- *Inventory*—Guardians must file a complete inventory of the property of the ward within 60 days of the appointment. Monthly income from Social Security and other pensions, etc. must be included.

- *Annual Accounting*—Every year, either upon the election of a fiscal year or between January 1 and April 1, a full record of receipts and disbursements must be filed with the court. A full accounting of all assets must be reported in the annual report. Failure of a Guardian to file this annual report may result in the Court's finding the Guardian in contempt and subject to removal as Guardian.

- *Close Transactions*—No Guardian shall purchase or borrow money from his ward.

- *Requirements for Sale or Exchange*—All sales or exchanges must be approved by the court. Guardians may petition the court for sale of the ward's property. The petition must include a brief statement of the reason for the proposed transaction, the name and address of the purchaser, and all other pertinent information. Finally, any knowledge of subsequent sales or transactions must be reported.

- *Appraisals*—No properties of the ward shall be sold unless properly appraised. Properties appraised longer than six months will generally have to be re-appraised. Properties usually cannot be sold through an appraiser of the estate.

- *Discharge*—Guardians should be discharged when the ward dies, is restored, or when a minor becomes 18 years of age. Guardians of property should also be discharged when assets are exhausted. Discharge proceedings should be initiated within 30 days of the above occurrences.

Guardianships of property may be avoided through the use of Living Trusts.

GUARDIANSHIP POWERS

Q. *What powers or authority do I have as Guardian in Florida without obtaining a court order?*

A. Close court supervision is required for all Guardianships but certain types of activities are permitted without a court order. The simplest rule to follow is to ask an attorney if there is any doubt. Generally a court order is not needed for the following matters:

1. Retention of assets owned by a ward, however, an inventory filed with the court is required.
2. Receipt of assets for the ward, however, an updated inventory is required.
3. Payment of ward's taxes and assessments.
4. Mortgage payments or payments of other "valid encumbrances." Any prepayment would require court approval.
5. Payment of reasonable living expenses for the ward, taking into consideration the standard of living, age, health, and financial circumstances of ward. Special rules apply to minors if their parents are financially able to meet certain maintenance and educational expenses, and the minor's assets may not be used for those reasons without court approval.
6. Exercising of the ward's right to elect to take the "elective share" or to exercise other rights in the estate of a deceased spouse.
7. Investing monies in a federally insured interest-bearing account, readily marketable secured loan arrangement, or other prudent investments.
8. Payment of expenses regarding the "administration of estate" as long as expenses were incidental in nature.
9. Decisions concerning the dissolution or reorganization of activities of a business enterprise.
10. Employment of agents to assist the guardian perform his duties when necessary.
11. Carrying out the orders of the court in performing guardianship duties.

It should be noted that several methods are available to avoid Guardianships and they include but are not limited to, "durable Family Powers of Attorney" and various types of "Trusts."

Careful consideration must be given before executing these instruments because many of the activities they allow can occur without court supervision.

Careful consideration should also be exercised when setting up joint accounts with children or other parties, as joint accounts have hidden dangers that should be discussed with your attorney.

GUARDIANSHIP POWERS

Q. *When do I have to get court approval in my role as Guardian?*

A. Many activities can be carried out without court order approval but under court supervision. Those activities requiring court orders are listed below.

- Whenever the Guardian chooses not to continue a contractual obligation or perform some activity that the ward had committed to, a court order is necessary.
- Performance or execution of any power that the incompetent could have completed, if competent.
- Improvement or extraordinary repairs, demolitions of buildings.
- The acceptance of any lease entered into for the ward.
- The abandonment of any property requires court approval.
- Any loan or pledging of assets as security.
- Sale, mortgage, or lease of any properties of the ward or for the use of the ward or family.
- Continuation of any partnership or any other business venture on behalf of the ward.
- Execution or continuation of any insurance payable to or for the benefit of the ward.
- Payment of funeral expenses and grave marker expenses for the ward.
- Gifting of the ward's property to members of the ward's family.
- Expenses involving estate and tax planning for the ward.

Any petition to sell property of the ward must include the necessity or expediency for the action, a description of the property to be sold, and the terms and price of the sale.

Guardianships require annual reportings to the court and annual inventory accounting. As you can determine from these writings, other accountings and court appearances are also necessary. Thus, there are continuing legal costs associated with the maintaining of a guardianship.

There are several steps which individuals can take to plan against being declared incompetent and avoid court appointed Guardians. These procedures should be discussed with an experienced attorney who can advise as to what protective features are necessary for proper estate administration.

REMOVAL OF GUARDIANS

Q. *Under what conditions may a guardian be removed or dismissed from his duties?*

A. Guardians may be removed for some of the following reasons:

1. Fraud in obtaining his appointment which includes falsification of statements on pleadings before the court;
2. Failure to discharge his duties as required by the court or failure to follow court rules or orders;
3. Abuse of his powers which covers many areas, but most often this occurs when Guardians act with self-interest and not in the best interest of the ward;
4. Insanity or other incompetency are grounds for removal of a guardian;
5. Prolonged sickness or excessive use of drugs or alcohol, preventing him from performing his duties;
6. Failure to account for items sold or provide schedules of sales of assets, or failure to produce the ward's assets when required to do so;
7. The wasting, embezzlement or mismanagement of assets;
8. Failure to file bond or give security when required by the court are grounds for dismissal;
9. Guardians can be dismissed when liquidators or receivers are appointed.

It should be noted that other penalties can be imposed in addition to dismissal for certain acts of a guardian.

The procedure for removal may be instituted by any interested party and the facts of the case must be stated by petition. A removed guardian must file a true, complete and final account of the property of the guardian within a specified time from his removal.

TRUSTS

LIVING TRUSTS

Many articles and books have been written which discuss the benefits of creating a Living Trust as the cornerstone of an individual's financial and estate plan. Unfortunately, not enough of this information has reached the average individual who has a great need for such benefits.

Q. *Who needs a Living Trust?*

A. All individuals and families should consider a Living Trust. Its primary advantage is to avoid the probate expense and probate delay at time of death. You should consult your attorney to discuss your particular needs in estate planning.

Q. *Can the owner of the Trust maintain complete control of the assets?*

A. Yes. Assets placed within a Living Trust can be retained under the complete management and control of the owner of such assets until he or she is ready to turn over the control to another individual or Trust company.

Q. *What happens to the Trust at time of sickness or incapacity of owner?*

A. The owner can set himself up as Trustee and direct that all of the funds of the Trust be used to provide for the financial and medical needs of the Trustee. Without this protection there is always the possibility of guardianship proceedings or delays in using the owner's assets for his own needs.

Q. *Is a Trust that is incorporated into a "Last Will and Testament" (Testamentary Trust) the same as a Living Trust?*

A. No. The property in the Will would have to be probated into the Trust and the cost of probation is very expensive and time consuming. This testamentary process, called probate, can be avoided for those assets placed into a Living Trust during the owner's lifetime.

Q. *What are the tax advantages of a Living Trust?*

A. This question does not have a simple answer. If one were to put all of his assets in a Living Trust the Trust would basically be taxed the same as the individual. However, thoughtful estate-planning attorneys often can set up Trusts that create thousands of dollars in tax savings.

Q. *What are the disadvantages of a Living Trust?*

A. Living Trusts do not go through probate and therefore the distribution of the estate is not approved by the court. Most Trusts cost at least $300 whereas Wills begin at $25. These items are minor when you consider the enormous savings and peace of mind a Trust can bring.

Q. *Why don't more families have Living Trusts?*

A. "Inertia and ignorance." Very few people take the time to fully understand the benefits of a Living Trust.

CRUMMEY TRUST

Q. *What is a Crummey Trust?*

A. The *Crummey* Trust has come to have a specific meaning for most estate planners. It is an inter vivos, irrevocable, unfunded life insurance Trust, gifts to which qualify for the annual gift tax exclusion.

To understand the *Crummey* Trust, one must have a general understanding of Trusts and be able to comprehend the terms in the above definition. A brief discussion of the key terms in the definition follows.

1. *Crummey*—Name of the family involved in the case upon which this concept is based. The court's decision marked the first judicial affirmation of the law in this area.
2. *Inter Vivos*—An Inter Vivos Trust is a Trust established by the grantor during his or her life.
3. *Irrevocable*—A Trust is irrevocable if, once established, it cannot be revoked, altered, or amended in any way.
4. *Unfunded*—One of the five requirements for a viable Trust is that it contain property. The Trust under consideration contains property in the form of life insurance policies.

    When estate planners talk about a funded Life Insurance Trust, they mean a Trust which not only contains life insurance policies, but other property as well, the income from which can be used to pay the premiums on the life insurance policies. Typically, the only property contained within a *Crummey* Trust is the policy of life insurance, and in that sense, it is "unfunded" because premiums must be provided from a source outside the Trust.
5. *Life Insurance*—Generally, the only asset of the Trust is life insurance on the life of the grantor.
6. *Qualifying for the Annual Gift Tax Exclusion*—Gifts to the Trust qualify for up to $5,000 of the $10,000 annual gift tax exclusion differentiating the *Crummey* Trust from other Inter Vivos Irrevocable Trusts.

CHARITABLE REMAINDER TRUST

Q. *Could you please explain the Charitable Remainder Trust and the benefits as it relates to estate planning?*

A. Federal tax laws make it possible to contribute sizable gifts without the loss of one's income. It is also possible to make large gifts to charity and actually increase one's lifetime spendable income in the process. This can all be made possible by creating a Charitable Remainder Trust.

The two types of Charitable Remainder Trusts are the *Annuity Trust* and the *Unitrust*. The Annuity Trust is one from which a specified sum is paid to the non-charitable beneficiary each year. With the Unitrust the net market value of its assets are determined annually. A prescribed percentage of this value is paid to the beneficiary each year and thus the payments may vary from year to year depending on the Trust's current asset value.

Under these Trusts the donor receives an immediate tax deduction for transferring assets to a Trust that meets the requirements of a charity under the Internal Revenue Code. A special provision should be included to the Trust allowing one to change the charitable beneficiary in case the charity receiving the gift ever loses its "charity status."

With the abundance of non-profit organizations emerging in the State of Florida, it becomes easy to do some estate planning which gives you favorable tax breaks and at the same time helps your favorite charity.

An example of how the Charitable Remainder Trust could work is as follows: Bob and Mary, age 75, owned stock in ABC Company which stock accelerated in value to $200,000.00. They decided to place this stock in a Charitable Remainder Trust and reserved for *themselves* a $15,000.00 annuity for the rest of their lives. They gave their assets upon death to their church, upon the death of the last survivor, Bob or Mary.

Because of their gift they avoided capital gains tax on the stock, increased their present level of income, and gained a huge tax deduction on their income for several years. They have a guaranteed source of income and have added more stability to their lives. Because of their religious beliefs, they are very content in knowing that their contribution will go for a needed purpose.

Trusts of this nature can be set up for any charitable organization recognized as such by the Internal Revenue Service.

As is the case in other Trusts, the Charitable Remainder Trust avoids *probate* of the assets attached to the Trust.

TESTAMENTARY TRUSTS

Q. *Do Testamentary Trusts avoid probate?*

A. No! All Wills are probated and Testamentary Trusts are created within Wills—thus assets devised in a Will to a Testamentary Trust would have to be probated. The fact that a Testamentary Trust has been created has not accomplished any avoidance of probate.

Testamentary Trusts serve a useful purpose in that they can be used as a tax-saving tool to divide large estates, and they can be a useful tool to keep persons from receiving an estate in one lump sum. Testamentary Trusts are also useful when beneficiaries are to receive "income only" monies.

If one has an interest in setting up a Trust that has all of the advantages of a Testamentary Trust *plus* avoid probate, then a exploration of the "Living Trust" should take place. Living Trusts are also known as Revocable Trusts, Family Trusts and a Grantor's Trust.

Living Trusts differ from Testamentary Trusts in that Living Trusts are established now while you are living, and you go through a personal (probate) proving process of your estate yourself without using the court process. This process is accomplished by keeping a Schedule "A" or inventory list of the items you have registered to the Trust. You never lose any power or control over any assets that you own in the Trust and you, yourself, serve as "Trustee" of the Trust.

A common myth about Living Trusts is that you lose control of your own property or that the Trust needs a tax number. Neither is true as no tax number is required and you don't lose any control of the assets.

The decision concerning whether one would want a Living Trust versus a Testamentary Trust will probably center around whether one would want his estate to be probated through the court system or whether one would rather bypass the probate system.

This discussion often centers around who the beneficiaries and Successor Trustees are. For example, if the Successor Trustees and beneficiaries are children, then many people desire to avoid probate and leave their entire estate probate free.

For those persons who had Testamentary Trusts drawn into their Wills before September of 1981, a thorough review of their documents should be analyzed by an attorney as the many tax changes that have taken place may have necessitated revisions to their documents.

For a thorough discussion of your estate planning needs, you should ask your attorney about "Trusts" for your estate.

ALIMONY TRUSTS

Q. *What is an Alimony Trust?*

A. An Alimony Trust can be a helpful settlement vehicle in divorce proceedings for a husband and wife with considerable assets. The advantages of such an arrangement would be the receipt of timely support payments plus a method to guarantee payment in the future.

An Alimony Trust is an excellent vehicle to use for the business owner where certain business assets that are producing income could be held in Trust. For example, if a business owner owned a corporation and the spouse did not feel comfortable with the owner's holding all the stock, the spouse's portion of the stock (to be received through a divorce proceeding) could be placed in an Alimony Trust with the spouse receiving the primary benefit from the stock.

Under the new tax rules, Alimony Trusts receive favorable tax considerations. The ultimate beneficiaries of this type Trust are usually the children, and the spouse's interest would terminate upon the spouse's death or remarriage. The Alimony Trust can also be set up to take care of child support payments or educational expenses for children, and again, can receive very favorable tax treatment under the new tax rules.

One of the most favorable tax changes has to do with how the "basis" of the property is established. Formerly, when property was transferred into an Alimony Trust, the IRS treated the transfer as a taxable event and a new basis assigned to whatever property was transferred into the Trust. The new tax rules allow that a taxable event does not occur and the tax basis of such a property does not change.

Annuity Trusts are also becoming a popular document in divorce planning. Such an instrument guarantees fixed monthly payments from the income and if the income is not sufficient, then payments would be deducted from the principal. Fixed income is a fairly dangerous concept so usually only a portion of the divorce property is placed in such an arrangement.

These types of Trusts are generally very similar to Trusts prepared in estate planning and offer the same benefits of:

1. Avoiding probate;
2. Avoiding six to twelve month or longer waiting period of probate;
3. Avoiding guardianship;
4. Providing for privacy.

It is also very important for divorced persons to consult an attorney to discuss their Will or Trust in order to assure that their estate will pass to their heirs, loved ones, or charities according to their wishes.

STAND-BY TRUSTS

Q. *What are Stand-By Trusts and how do they work?*

A. There are several different versions of this Trust. Some of them are as follows:

A Trust is created whereby no assets are put in the Trust, but the creator signs a power of attorney which directs someone of his choosing to put his assets in Trust upon the physical or mental incapacity of the creator.

The difficulty of this arrangement usually arises upon how the determination of incompetency is determined. Another difficulty would be if the creator died before his assets were placed in the Trust, as the assets would be probated thereby making the Trust worthless.

Another version of the Stand-By Trust is where a person transfers his property into a Trust and maintains control of the assets but has a Trustee take over upon his incapacity.

In some cases a Stand-By Trust has a Trustee take over the management of assets when the creator is going to be out of the country or out of town on an extended trip. The Successor Trustee then can manage the assets on a temporary or permanent basis.

The well-publicized Dacey Trust has characteristics of the Stand-By Trust. The Dacey Trust is a Revocable Trust where the creator of the Trust has a life interest in the Trust and powers to manage the assets himself. It provides for quick transfer of Trustees, fast distribution of assets upon death, avoidance of probate, privacy and avoidance of some guardianship possibilities.

Florida Trusts can be drafted to accomplish the same distributions of assets as provided for in a Last Will and Testament. If properly drafted, the assets can be distributed immediately upon death and not go through the probate system.

The use of Stand-By Trusts can be an effective estate planning tool, but caution should be exercised in any delay of placing assets in Trust once the Trust has been created. The Trust, just as Testamentary Trusts (Trusts created by Wills), would not be a useful tool if the creator died before the assets were placed in Trust.

RABBI TRUST

Q. *Can a person be taxed on gifts to a Trust for his benefit?*

A. In a recent Internal Revenue Service ruling the answer would appear to be "no" under certain conditions.

The IRS ruled that an Irrevocable Trust established for a rabbi did not cause the rabbi to be taxed on the assets transferred to the Trust. The IRS ruled that there was neither a taxable economic benefit to the rabbi nor constructive receipt of the proceeds. The Trust that was set up was also subject to the claims of creditors of the congregation who established the Trust.

The Trust for the rabbi further stated that the Trustees would manage, invest, and reinvest the Trust estate and pay the income derived from the Trust to the rabbi every three months. Upon the rabbi's death, disability, retirement or termination of services, the Trustees would make distributions of principal and income to the rabbi as provided for in the Trust agreement. The congregation was not allowed to alter, amend, revoke, change or annul any provisions of the Trust agreement.

After reviewing the terms of the Trust, the IRS decided that the gifts made to the Trust would not be taxable to the rabbi but only the income from the Trust would be taxable. The main reasons that the principal was not taxable was because the Trust was Irrevocable and the Trust assets were subject to the congregation's creditors. Any principal paid to the rabbi from the Trust would be taxable as received by the rabbi or as otherwise made available.

Trusts such as the one described above are unusual and out of the ordinary. Irrevocable Trusts are normally used only in specific and unique circumstances. Most Trusts are revocable and amendable and can be excellent tools in estate planning. The most common name for these type Trusts are inter vivos or "Living Trusts" and should be considered in any estate where the goals are avoiding probate, planning guardianship, privacy and quick finalization of an estate.

FLORIDA LAND TRUSTS

Q. *What are the benefits of a Florida Land Trust?*

A. One of the main benefits of a Florida Land Trust is that of privacy. One can own and control land without it becoming a matter of public record. Walt Disney World was acquired through separate purchases using Land Trusts.

In order to provide privacy, the owner must choose a Trustee who would hold title to the land. Beneficiaries may be named in the Trust document although they do not have to be named.

Land Trusts avoid probate as do other types of Trusts in Florida. Probate costs average 3%-10% of the market value of land if left by a Will. Also, an estate of a person owning multiple pieces of land in multiple states will go through multiple probate proceedings unless the land is held in some type of Trust. It may also be possible to avoid giving a spouse a forced or statutory share if the property is held in Trust and such an arrangement is not usually available through a Will.

Land Trusts can be a help in keeping liens and judgments off properties. Judgments and liens do not attach to the land held in a Trust. It is unclear in Florida how a creditor could sue the beneficiary of a Land Trust.

If several people own a property or properties, it may be advantageous for them to maintain the property in a Land Trust and allow a Trustee to handle all the transactions instead of each owner having to sign each and every document regarding the property. If the primary concern is secrecy, it is usually better for the person who is actually purchasing the property to do so in the name of the Trust rather than a present owner transferring it into a Land Trust. The reason for this is that if a present owner transferred his property to a Land Trust, that transfer would indicate the owner of record.

Another benefit of the Florida Land Trust is that land in Trusts are not able (generally) to be partitioned. Land held other than in Trust can be partitioned through the courts, if requested by a disgruntled owner. Trust language should in most cases prohibit partition to avoid legal hassles between joint owners.

Florida Land Trusts do not create additional tax filings other than a disclosure form known as Form 56.

YOUR LIVING TRUST

Q. *What is a Living Trust?*

A. I like to explain a Living Trust as being no more than a fancy Will that has some special features. Those special features are: (1) avoiding probate; (2) quick distribution; (3) guardianship plan; and (4) privacy. A typical Trust would have many of the following provisions:

Opening Paragraph: The opening paragraph usually names the *Grantors* (persons creating the Trust) and the *Trustees* (persons managing the Trust). In most cases the Trustee and Grantor are the same person. The Successor Trustees are also named and they are usually your primary beneficiaries, your bank, or your attorney. Your attorney and you can decide which choice best suits your situation.

Witnesseth: Trusts generally have a "contract" paragraph which states that the Grantor and Trustee (both you) agree to create a Trust and agree to place assets in the Trust and list those assets on a "Schedule A". Schedule A is a list of the assets that are placed into the Trust. You may place all of your assets into a Trust.

Grantor's Life Interest: The Grantors usually reserve a life interest in the Living Trust for themselves. This is accomplished by stating that they may use the principal and income for themselves and that even if incapacitated, the principal and income must be used for their benefit.

Distribution: The distribution paragraph of a Trust is almost identical to that of a Will. You may leave your estate to whomever you wish and those persons are listed in this paragraph along with what percentage of the estate they will receive.

Retention of Minor Beneficiary Interest: This paragraph states that any minor cannot receive a distribution until he or she has reached the age of 18 or 21 (or older), but the monies may be used for college, education, maintenance or proper support.

Spendthrift Provision: A spendthrift provision states that the Trust shall be free from control or interference from any *spouse* of a married beneficiary and a beneficiary shall not have the power to pledge, assign or encumber his or her interest or be subject to any debts or obligations of any type.

Trustee Powers: The Trustees reserve for themselves all of the powers that they had before they created the Trust. Generally they are to sell, lease, mortgage, invest, vote on proxies, keep unproductive assets, make distributions in kind, determine what is income and principal, determine how to hold title, withdraw payments, buy margin accounts or options, and to exercise all powers and discretions given to a Trustee under Florida law.

Duties of Trustees: Trustees have a duty to file any required income tax, intangible tax and see that any taxes are paid thereon. Trustees have a duty to maintain record of receipts and disbursements.

Succession of Trustees: Upon the death, resignation or incapacity of any active Trustee the next Successor Trustee shall take over the duties of Trustee. A clause is usually added that would determine what constitutes the incapacity of a Trustee to act.

Trustees Resignation: You can't make a Trustee be a Trustee if the individual does not wish to be. Therefore, you give instructions as to how a Trustee would resign. Trustees must follow this procedure before the next Trustee would assume the position.

Exoneration for Duty to Audit: Formal audits are not usually required and Trustees may assume their duty without such audit.

Rule Against Perpetuities: A complex area of the law but generally no Trust should be created that shall defer the vesting of any interest beyond 21 years after the death of the last to die of the beneficiaries.

Non-Liability of Third Parties: This clause serves as a release for banks, transfer agents, etc. who follow your instructions by relying upon provisions in the Trust. This clause also provides for "signatories" to be authorized.

Terms: Most Trusts have a glossary which defines words such as children, issue, rule against perpetuities, etc.

Payment of Taxes and Expenses: Trustees must pay all debts and expenses plus all taxes before they make a distribution of the assets. They are also instructed to make necessary elections regarding filing taxes and are exonerated from making tax elections.

Governing Law: The Trust is generally governed by the laws in all respects of the state in which it was created.

Amendment and Revocation: One of the most important clauses is that the Trust may be amended, changed, or revoked at any time by the Grantor.

Special Clauses: Any number of special clauses may be added to fit the special needs of the Grantor.

A Living Trust can be an excellent tool in planning one's estate. You should consult your attorney to see if it fits your needs. The attorney you choose should be familiar with Trusts in estate planning.

LIVING TRUST:
ANSWER TO ARCHAIC PROBATE SYSTEM

Q. *I have recently attended several financial planning seminars and have developed a great deal of interest in "Living Trusts." Why don't more attorneys explain to people the advantages of a Living Trust vs. a Will?*

A. You have asked a very good question that is difficult to answer. One attorney cannot speak for other attorneys.

Generally speaking, attorneys that primarily prepare Wills for their clients can develop a large probate practice. Probate is very distasteful to me primarily because it takes a long time before beneficiaries (other than the husband or wife) can receive any distribution of the estate; attorney fees and personal representative fees take up a portion of the estate. Wills do nothing to avoid guardianship problems and Wills become a part of the county's public records disclosing the testator's assets to anyone that has an interest. All of this can be avoided with a Living Trust.

The most common reasons for not having a Living Trust are ill-advised: (1) losing control of assets in Trust; (2) improper management of assets; (3) expense of Trust; (4) additional tax ID number for Trust. *NONE* of these are true because the Trustee (you) have complete control of all the assets in Trust, and you manage the assets in the Trust the very same as you do individually, and tax ID numbers are no longer required. Trust prices vary and are inexpensive compared to the high cost of probate. A Living Trust has absolutely no disadvantages.

The advantages of a Trust are:

- Income from the Trust will continue upon death without delay and expense of probate;
- Life insurance may be payable to the Trust;
- Assets upon death may immediately be distributed in a Trust as opposed to six months to one year or longer in a Will;
- Trusts can be terminated without cost;
- Successor Trustees may be given powers to pay doctor and hospital bills (nothing happens in a Will until death);
- Investments and financial decisions can be decided while you are alive to save loved ones from making unwise and untimely decisions after your death;
- Guardianship problems are avoided;
- You may save federal estate and income taxes through the use of a Trust;
- Trust provisions can be changed at any time;
- Payments out of the principal of your estate may be made at any time;

If you desire a professional Trustee to manage your estate and Trust, you can receive a monthly check and you may travel freely and your checks sent to any part of the world.

Estate planning is not complete without a very thorough discussion with your attorney about a "Living Trust." It is indeed a very modern instrument that is an answer to the somewhat archaic probate system.

TO TRUST OR NOT TO TRUST

Q. *Can you explain the various different types of Trusts in estate planning and the best approach in selecting one for avoiding taxes and probate?*

A. Trusts are often used in estate planning and their advantages are secrecy, avoidance of federal tax, and avoidance of probate costs. Wills become a matter of public record along with guardianships, and thus are not secretive at all. Wills also take up to a year, or longer to probate at considerable cost to the estate. The primary difficulty and disadvantage of Trusts are their complexity to understand, their difficulty to properly manage and the higher cost to establish.

The higher cost to establish a Trust is insignificant compared to the cost and time delay of a Will. The complexity and managing of the assets should be left to your estate planning team of at least two of the following individuals: Certified Financial Planner, Certified Public Accountant, Insurance Agent and your attorney. The best combination is an attorney or CPA experienced in estate planning *and* a certified financial planner or insurance agent qualified in estate planning. It usually costs the same, but the benefits are much greater if you use a specialist in the estate planning area.

DIFFERENT TYPES OF TRUSTS

TESTAMENTARY TRUST—Created in the Grantor's/Trustee's Will. This type of Trust does not avoid probate as all of the assets in the Will are probated. Since these types of Trusts are usually subject to the ongoing jurisdiction of the probate court, they are often called *Court Trusts*.

LIVING TRUSTS—are also called Inter Vivos Trusts. They are created during one's life and are completely revocable during one's lifetime. Assets can be added or deleted during the life of the Trust and grantor. Living Trusts generally avoid probate and assets in the Trust can be passed very quickly upon death. Living Trusts are not subject to the jurisdiction of the court.

LIFE INSURANCE TRUSTS—are Living Trusts and the proceeds of an insurance policy are left to a Trust normally so a Trustee can distribute the monies according to a plan so the money may be more wisely spent or reserved for a longer period of time.

CHARITABLE TRUST—is simply a Trust which has a charity as its beneficiary.

ACCUMULATION TRUST—This Trust accumulates income and is not distributed as income until some later time when it may be distributed as principal.

IRREVOCABLE TRUST—Just like it sounds, an Irrevocable Trust may never be changed, never amended, never revoked. The terms of the Trust are permanent. These types of Trusts are generally only used under special circumstances.

BY-PASS TRUST—This is a Trust where husband (x) and wife (y) form a Trust and when x dies y receives the income from the Trust as long as y may live with the principal of the Trust being disbursed to the children at the time of the death of y. Such Trusts can be structured to avoid estate tax and make maximum contribution to the children.

CLIFFORD TRUST—Clifford Trusts are Irrevocable Trusts that specify that the income from whatever property is put into the Trust shall be paid to a beneficiary other than the Trustor or his spouse for a period in excess of ten years, and therefore the property is to revert to the Trustor. If the beneficiary is in a much lower income tax bracket than is the Trustor, a large amount of income taxes may be saved each year over the ten year period, compared to what the Trustor would have paid in his own tax bracket.

TOTTEN TRUSTS—Totten Trusts are also known as "Poor Man's Wills." A good example of a Totten Trust would be when a grandfather opens an account with his own funds "as Trustee" for his grandson. The grandfather will have total control over the funds in the account, but they pass probate-free to the grandson at the grandfather's death.

LIFETIME GIVING—The annual gift tax exclusion has been raised to $10,000 per person per year. This may provide all the tax reduction a given estate may wish. If one had an estate of $500,000 and ten donees available, he could give his estate away over five years (10 donees x $10,000 x 5 years = $500,000). Also, if one is giving away property at today's prices, one is also giving away *appreciation*. Gifting can be very advantageous to the overall estate plan.

A-B TRUST—Before the 1981 Reagan tax cut, the A-B Marital Trust was quite common. The 1976 tax law allowed one-half of the estate or $250,000 whichever was greater to pass tax free into one Trust and the residue to pass into a residuary Trust which was taxable. It is very possible that this type Trust is not applicable in the larger estates today.

TRUST POWER

Q. *Do I lose control of my assets if I place them in a "Living Trust"?*

A. No. This is a common misunderstanding about the use of Living Trusts in estate planning. The fear of "losing control" is without merit.

A clause usually found in the Trust agreement is called "Grantor's Life Interest". This clause usually directs that the income and principal *must* be used for the benefit of the Grantor (person creating the Trust) as long as he/she lives.

The income or principal of the Trust can be spent exactly as though the assets were owned individually even though they are now in the Trust.

For example, if husband and wife created a Living Trust and the husband died and the wife later became incompetent, the Successor Trustee(s) (named by the Grantors) are directed by the Trust to manage the assets for the wife's (Grantor) interest for as long as she may live. It is entirely possible that if the husband and wife had placed most of their assets in the Trust that incompetency proceedings in court could be avoided.

In order for the Successor Trustee(s) to take over bank accounts and stocks, etc., the Trust usually provides that the Successor Trustee can provide the statements of two licensed doctors of medicine to establish the incapacity of the Grantor to act in his/her own behalf. The Trust in this case has made it possible for Successor Trustee(s) to take over assets without a court hearing and approval from the court on expenditures.

Successor Trustee(s) can resign at any time in most Trust agreements by giving 30 day notice to the beneficiaries and other Successor Trustee(s) can take over. Thus, if the Grantors have named their children as first, second and third Successor Trustees, and after the husband and wife have died or became incompetent and the first successor is then unable to perform the duties of Trustee, then he may resign and the second successor may take over. If all three successors cannot perform the duties of Successor Trustee, then they and the beneficiaries may appoint a Trustee.

In summary, the person(s) creating a "Living Trust" do not lose power or control of the assets they place in the Trust. They have absolutely the same control over the assets in the Trust as they do over assets owned individually. By creating a Trust they have also controlled who would manage the assets if they were to become incapacitated in any way.

ADMINISTERING ASSETS TO A TRUST

Q. *My husband recently died. Over fifteen years ago we paid a substantial amount of money to an attorney to create a "Living Trust" to avoid probate. Most of our assets were held by my husband. Now my attorney is going to charge a substantial probate fee because the assets were never attached to the Trust. What happened?*

A. Unfortunately, your situation is fairly common. Living Trusts to most people are "new" and complex to understand. Your attorney probably told you to attach your assets to the "Schedule A" of the Trust and you never understood what a "Schedule A" was or the importance of it to the Trust. A "Schedule A" is a list of assets that *you* maintain, keeping a record of the items you place in your Trust as Trustee.

A brief outline of the things you should do after the Trust is created is as follows:

1. Make sure you thoroughly understand each and every provision of your Trust and the associated benefits. Ask your attorney to read aloud parts of the document that you don't understand and explain them to you.
2. Make a copy of your Trust for your bank(s). Your banker will register all of your accounts to the Trust.
3. Take a copy of your Trust to your securities dealer and he or she will register all of your stocks to the Trust.
4. If you are working with a certified financial planner he/she can often re-register all of your assets to the Trust for a very modest charge.

5. Your insurance should be analyzed as an important part of your estate and you should have the opinion of any two of the following people concerning insurance and your estate:
    (a) Estate attorney;
    (b) CPA (knowledgeable in estates)
    (c) Insurance person (qualified in estates)
    (d) Certified Financial Planner
6. Real property can be easily deeded to the Trust. You should consult with an attorney so that homestead rights will not be affected.
7. Cars, trucks, RV's and other vehicles can be registered to the Trust by simply having the title registered in the name of the Trust. However, this procedure is not always recommended and you should consult your attorney.
8. Valuable personal property, i.e. expensive jewelry, fur coats, etc. can be attached to the Trust by including them on the "Schedule A."

Although these steps sound time consuming, they are easy to do and uncomplicated. All of the steps can be accomplished in a few hours. The net result of a Trust will be avoidance of probate charges (2%-10% of your total estate), avoidance of guardianship problems, maintaining secrecy as opposed to a Will's public record exposure, and passing the estate in a very short period of time in contrast to a Will's very long period of time.

WILL OR TRUST PROVISIONS FOR BUSINESS OWNERS

Q. *What provisions should I be concerned about in my Will if I own a business?*

A. The answer to your question depends on what type of business you own.

A good partnership agreement should be in writing and detailed and specific enough to describe exactly what would happen upon the death of one of the partners.

A buy-sell agreement is especially helpful for business owners and particularly helpful if a corporation is involved. A price per share can be established and modified on a yearly or bi-yearly basis.

Where it is not practicable to control a business interest in the estate plan with a buy-sell agreement, special provisions must be made in the owner's Will. In addition to actually disposing of the business interest itself, the following basic administrative clauses must be considered if applicable to the particular case:

- A clause that specifically authorizes the personal representative or Trustee to continue the business operation, if the client so wishes. It should authorize to incorporate the business, to borrow funds, or possibly to sell, merge, or acquire other business, if practical.

- If the business is already incorporated, it might be appropriate to include a power that gives the personal representative the authority to reorganize, interact with management, vote in voting Trust plans, and trade stock in merger plans.
- The personal representative or Trustee should also be authorized to pay any appropriate taxes concerning the business.

A consideration of a business owner should be to hold his business interest in a Trust. A Trust could avoid the lengthy delay and expense of probate and keep the business operating on a smooth and uninterrupted schedule.

Another important consideration in business planning should be key man insurance and insurance funding for a buy-sell agreement.

DURABLE FAMILY POWER OF ATTORNEY

Q. *Of what use is a "Durable Family Power of Attorney" and how is it different from a "Power of Attorney?"*

A. Perhaps the best way to answer this question is to simplify a sample "Durable Family Power of Attorney" and let you see the usefulness of the document. A *partial* excerpt would read as follows:

KNOW ALL MEN BY THESE PRESENTS THAT (husband) (hereinafter referred to as "Grantor") has made (wife) his true and lawful attorney for "Grantor" and in "Grantor's" name, place and stead to make, execute, sign, endorse or deliver any and all documents in "Grantor's" name, or on behalf of "Grantor", without reservation or limitation, it being "Grantor's" intention to hereby comply with and extend all of the authority contained in Chapter 709.08, Florida Statutes.

This durable family power of attorney shall not be affected by disability of "Grantor", except as provided by statute, and shall continue in full force and effect unless and until revoked by "Grantor" in writing, or terminated by law or the lawful order of a court of competent jurisdiction. This power of attorney shall be nondelegable and shall cease upon death of "Grantor". All acts performed hereunder by attorney shall bind "Grantor" and the heirs, devisees and personal representatives of "Grantor".

Said attorney(s) are hereby given and granted full power and authority to do and perform all and every act and thing whatsoever requisite and necessary to be done in and about the premises as fully, to all intents and purposes, as

"Grantor" might or could do it personally present, hereby ratifying and confirming all that "Grantor's" said attorney(s) shall lawfully do or cause to be done by virtue hereof.

It is obvious that the Durable Family Power of Attorney goes beyond the "General Power of Attorney" by giving family members special powers in time of disability.

NOTE: This article should not be used in attempting to draft your own "Durable Family Power of Attorney." You should consult your attorney for proper *format* and *execution.* Attorney fees are usually very nominal for this type of service.

TRUST BURDENS

Q. *Do Living Trusts generate additional reporting requirements and additional tax forms?*

A. In general terms, the answer to your question is no. The Internal Revenue Service used to require a tax number for Trusts, but that is no longer required. Such tax numbers made it necessary to file a 1041 tax form. There are some circumstances where taxpayers use the Trusts very much like a corporation and additional tax numbers may be required. In most cases the IRS treats the individual and the Trust as the same person and only the individual's social security number is used as a tax number.

As a practical example, suppose a husband and wife created a Trust to avoid the probating of their assets. As they "register" their bank account to the Trust they only need to use their social security number as the tax number for the Trust. When their Trust receives a 1099 form, it will show up on the individual's social security or tax number. The information on the 1099 form gets reported on the 1040 (the same as usual). In this example the only thing that has changed is that the husband and wife have created a Trust that has saved their estate thousands of dollars. No additional "tax" work has been created.

As a person registers stocks, bonds, and other securities to the Trust, the same procedure is used. The social security number of the creator of the Trust is used which avoids additional tax work.

Real estate holdings can also be placed into a Living Trust and because the Trust and the person are treated the same, no additional tax concerns are generated.

Most Trusts have a clause which "exonerates the duty to audit." This clause allows a Successor Trustee to take over the management of a Trust without auditing the activities of the "Grantor" Trustee. Such provisions also alleviate additional paperwork that could be associated with Trusts.

In summary, Trusts can be drafted so that no additional tax work, audits, or reports become necessary.

TRUST LITIGATION

Q. *Can a Living Trust be contested in the same manner as a Will can be contested?*

A. An Inter-Vivos "Living" Trust, also known as a self-directed Grantor's Trust, can be contested but not in the same exact manner as a Will would be contested.

Wills are contested in the probate court; and whereas Trusts do not have to be probated, they are generally handled as a civil matter and litigation would occur in civil court. As a matter of law, Trusts can be compared to contracts and are treated in a similar manner.

Trusts may be challenged for some of the following reasons:

LACK OF CAPACITY

The requirements for creating a Will or a Trust are similar under Florida law in that the one creating the document has to have "testamentary capacity" and the instrument must be executed by a competent party and pertain to a lawful subject matter.

As an interesting observation, there is a 1980 Florida case in which medical testimony was rejected and lay testimony was accepted regarding the testamentary capacity of a testator.

UNDUE INFLUENCE

A Trust may be set aside if it was procured by undue influence. Most case law concerning undue influence exists where there has been a confidential relationship between a decedent and the one who has actually procured the gift.

The courts in these cases allow evidence as to why the gifts were made and allow explanations as to why the person alleged to have performed the undue influence was involved in the affairs of the decedent. Undue influence also includes over-persuasion, duress, force, coercion, or artful or fraudulent contrivance to such a degree that there is a destruction of the free agency and will power of the one making the Trust.

FRAUD

A Trust may be invalidated if elements of fraud have taken place. Many of the elements of undue influence and each aspect of capacity can be intertwined in fraud with regards to Trust preparation.

Perhaps the most common elements of fraud is "fraud in the inducement" which means that one was coerced or tricked into creating a Trust for the benefit of someone else. As in undue influence, the most important consideration is whether there was a contrivance to such a degree that there is a destruction of the free agency and will power of the one making the Trust.

MISTAKE

Mistake in the inducement to execute or to amend a Trust is not commonly a sufficient ground for invalidating a Trust. In other words, the courts will not generally set aside a Trust if it were created or changed on a false belief, but it could consider arguments that the Trust was created with "mistakes" in the contents of the Trust.

CONTRAVENTION OF PUBLIC POLICY

A violation of public policy is usually sufficient to prevent the carrying out of the purposes of a Trust.

UNDERPRODUCTIVE PROPERTY

Q. *My Living Trust has a clause which states that the Trustee may without regard to any statute or rule of law not be bound to Florida Statute 738.12 concerning underproductive property. Why?*

A. Your Trust has a clause that is very common in Florida Trusts. First, it is important to define underproductive property. It can generally be defined as property which does not earn at least three percent income per year.

Under Florida Statute, Trustees must pay income-beneficiaries an amount equal to three percent of the value of the principal, based on the market value at the end of the calendar year. If the total income does not equal three percent, then payments must be made from the principal.

Although three percent sounds like an extremely low number, it can become a great administrative nuisance to a Trustee. For example, a Trustee who has to manage a large portfolio of stocks, without being exempt from the statute, may have to certify that each stock met the "3% test." With the clause added to your Trust this will not be necessary. Although stocks not earning three percent may not be thought worth holding at first, there are many growth oriented stocks (low income) and closely-held corporations which may fail to meet the test. It is also possible that tracts of vacant land may not earn three percent income in a given year which could cause the land to be sold.

As you can tell, it is very possible that your portfolio of assets has underproductive property and that your Successor Trustees should be protected from the administrative hassles of dealing with the problem. The problem is easily alleviated by adding the clause which you questioned.

Another common statute from which Trustees can be exempt is Florida Statute 738.07 which generally states that any receipt by reason of ownership of a bond is classified as income. Thus the Trustee is not required to reduce or increase this type of receipt to account for any premium or discount paid for the bond when an interest payment is received.

It should be obvious that Trusts should not be attempted by the do-it-yourselfers. Trust planning requires an experienced practitioner that considers the size of the estate, the mixture of assets, tax ramifications, potential beneficiary problems and what statutes, if any, should be exempt from your Trust. Many other factors could be important in your estate plan.

COMMON MISCONCEPTIONS
ABOUT LIVING TRUSTS

Q. *I have recently had a Living Trust prepared and comments from friends have caused me concern. Why are there so many misconceptions about Trusts?*

A. Misconceptions concerning Trusts occur frequently probably because people tend to ask everyone *but* a competent estate or Trust attorney their questions about Living Trusts. Some of the most common misconceptions of Trusts are the following:

1. Trusts have special tax numbers.
   FALSE per Regulation 1.6012-3(a)(9).
2. Special reports and tax returns have to be filed.
   FALSE per Regulation 1.6012-3(a)(9).
3. Depletion allowance for minerals is lost.
   FALSE per Letter Ruling 8104202.
4. Trust administration is difficult.
   FALSE. This is false in most cases, however, some cases may need a professional Trustee and legal assistance may be needed to transfer properties and mortgages. Professional help may also be needed to file tax returns on large estates.
5. Trusts mean giving up control of the assets.
   FALSE. The person setting up the Trust maintains full control.
6. Banks or Trust departments must serve as the Trustee.
   FALSE. The Trustee may be yourself and other members of your family. This choice is *yours*.
7. Trust assets cannot be invaded as to principal.
   FALSE. Trust assets may be invaded, but under the supervision and guidance of competent estate counsel.

8. Merger defeats the Trust where the Grantor, Trustee and current beneficiary are the same person.

   FALSE. Merger—The grantor can be the sole Trustee as long as there is at least one other beneficiary, either present or future, to prevent merger of the legal and equitable interests and termination of the Trust. The fact that the Grantor may terminate the interest of the other beneficiaries by revoking the Trust does not eliminate their interests for purpose of the doctrine of merger.

9. Trusts are for large estates.

   FALSE. Trusts can be for any size estate.

10. Homestead exemptions will be lost if the property is placed in Trust.

    FALSE. A competent estate and Trust attorney will assist you in keeping your homestead exemption.

11. Business interests cannot be held in Trust.

    FALSE. All business interests can be held in Trust.

The principal advantages of a Living Trust over a Will are (1) avoiding probate, (2) faster in distribution of assets, (3) guardianship planning to avoid being declared incompetent, (4) privacy.

TRUST AMENDMENTS

Q. *Can a "Living Trust" be amended?*

A. Yes, it is common to amend a Trust from time to time as circumstances change. Some reasons for Trust amendments are as follows:

1. Changes in the number of family members either by birth, death, divorce or marriage;
2. Changes in relationships within the family group;
3. Changes in financial or economic conditions;
4. Change of circumstances or need of a beneficiary such as disability, handicap, or special education needs that occurred since the creation of the Trust;
5. New interests in charitable or education institutions;

The most common provisions in a Trust that are amended are as follows:

1. The preference or order of Trustees;
2. The distribution of the assets of the Trust estate;
3. Additional provisions for grandchildren's education or other special needs;

4. The preference of contingent beneficiaries upon the death of any of the primary beneficiaries;

5. Change of any restrictive powers that may be listed in the Trust.

Q. *What changes are necessary if I move to another state in my "Living Trust"?*

A. A simple amendment changing the situs of the Trust and changing the "Article" which states the Trust shall be governed by the laws of the State of _____, is usually all that is necessary.

Living Trusts should also be changed if there are tax laws that have been passed that would change the tax status of your estate. All Trusts created before September 1981 should be reviewed especially if they recite prior tax provisions of the Internal Revenue Code. Failure to amend Trusts dated before September 1981 could result in the Trust being taxed upon death of the Grantor at a higher rate than necessary.

As a general rule you should not have more than two amendments to a Trust document at any one time. If more than two amendments have taken place, you should consider consolidating the amendments or possibly creating one document which would restate the entire wishes and desires that you desire to achieve.

Trusts and their amendments should be reviewed every two years. Of particular importance is the review of the "Schedule A" or list of assets placed in the Trust. If a Trust has been prepared and the assets have not been placed in the Trust, or if they have been removed, the purpose of the Trust will not be realized.

One of the most common reasons for not creating a Trust is not true. Most people think that a Trust is a rigid, inflexible document that cannot be changed. As you have read, this is false as it is very easy to amend a Trust at anytime by simply preparing a Trust Amendment.

TRUSTS AND HOMESTEAD EXEMPTIONS

Q. *Can I place my home in a "Living Trust" and maintain my homestead exemption?*

A. Yes, you may place your homestead in a Living Trust and maintain your exemption. In order to qualify for the homestead exemption one must have a clearly defined vested possessory right to the property.

Florida law allows an exemption from taxation to every person who has legal or equitable title to real estate and uses said estate as his permanent home. Of course, other requirements have to be met, but one of the most important factors in determining homestead is how title is held. When property is placed into a Living Trust, the legal title is generally held by the Trustee. If the Trustee used the property as a homestead and meets all the other requirements, the property would qualify for the homestead exemption.

In order for a Trustee to qualify for the exemption, he must have a clearly defined vested possessory right to the property. This right may be established in either the Trust document itself or established in the deed which conveys the property to the Trust.

If the intent of the attorney is to establish this right in the conveyance (deed), language such as "the property is held in Trust for the use and benefit of the Trustee," would be sufficient to reserve the homestead. Other language that reserves the homestead would be to add FBO (for benefit of) the Trustee's name and/or to add "for the sole use and benefit of (the Trustee). Sometimes the words, "The Grantor reserves his homestead rights," is typed on the deed.

Language that is acceptable in the Trust instrument creating equitable title would be a provision such as, "Subject to the other terms of this instrument, X is entitled to possession of the property described as (legal description)."

In summary, the creation of a Trust and the conveyance of property into the Trust *DOES NOT* affect your homestead exemption if properly handled. An attorney familiar with creating Trusts and handling real estate will take the proper steps to reserve your homestead exemption while keeping your property out of probate.

NON-TAXABLE TRUSTS

Q. *Are Living Trusts taxable?*

A. If a Living Trust is created for the sole use and benefit of the maker (grantor), it is not recognized as a separate tax entity, and the Trust is therefore non-taxable. The grantor would report the income in this situation on his personal tax return (1040) in the same manner as though the Trust was never created.

It is a common myth that those who create a Trust are responsible to file a separate tax return and keep separate tax records. This was true several years ago, but the Internal Revenue Service has since dropped any such requirement. The grantor is deemed as the owner of the assets.

The maker (grantor) is treated as owner if the income is either: 1) Distributed, actually or constructively, to the grantor or grantor's spouse; 2) Assets and/or income are held for future distribution to the grantor or grantor's spouse; 3) Income is used for the payment of premiums on life insurance policies.

As most readers know, there is no Florida income tax on natural persons as it is forbidden by the Florida Constitution. Florida does, however, tax corporations which leads many persons to think that Trusts are taxed separately in the state of Florida. This is not true, as the state of Florida specifically excludes private Trusts, Inter Vivos Trusts, i.e. "Living Trusts."

Trusts can be effectively used to reduce or eliminate Federal Estate tax. The Economic Recovery Tax Act increased the amount of the unified estate and gift tax to $192,000 in 1987, which is the equivalent of passing $600,000 tax free in 1987. There is an effective way to leave up to $1,200,000 tax free with help from a competent estate planning counsel.

Florida does not have an estate tax on estates, however, if the size of the estate would make it taxable on the federal level, the state of Florida would receive a portion of the tax dollar received by the federal government.

The Florida intangible personal property tax does not effect those natural persons who have created a Trust any differently than if they did not have a Trust. In other words, the intangible tax would be the same with or without a Trust.

In summary, the creation of a Living Trust in which the maker (grantor) reserves a life interest in the assets of the Trust is not effected any differently than if the Trust was never created—his taxes are exactly the same. Substantial federal estate tax savings can be achieved through the use of multiple Trusts.

TRUST ACCOUNTINGS

Q. *I have a Living Trust. Upon my death is my Successor Trustee accountable to my beneficiaries?*

A. Yes. Florida statutes state that a *vested* Trust beneficiary is entitled to an annual accounting or an accounting upon the termination of the Trust or the death of one of the Trustees. Contingent beneficiaries are no longer entitled to any type of accounting. It is generally thought that this duty and obligation cannot be waived, although it is quite common to do so. Florida statutes further state that a beneficiary is barred from contesting or making a claim against the Trustee six months after receipt of an accounting.

One of the advantages of a Living Trust is the privacy feature. Florida law states that Trust accountings *do not* have to be filed with the circuit court. Upon a dispute between the Trustees and/or beneficiaries, the court does have the power to review the accountings if an action is commenced in court. The court, of course, does not have continuing power of supervision of the Trust.

Current law does not specify the exact form in which accountings must be presented. A minimum requirement would be:

1. A beginning inventory (description of assets);
2. Statement of receipts;
3. Statement of disbursements;
4. Ending inventory.

An accounting should be "self-proving" if it is self-balancing.

It should be noted that the Grantor (creator of the Trust), who in most cases is also the Trustee, is not required to account to anyone of what he does with his own assets while he is living. This subject matter only regards the functions and duties of the Successor Trustee upon the death of the Grantor. It should be noted that under a Trust agreement, Successor Trustees have similar duties to those of a personal representative of a Will. The primary difference is that assets in a Trust do not have to go through the "probate court" system. The Successor Trustee may need some assistance from an attorney or accountant, but the cost of this service should be significantly less than if the whole estate had to go through the probate system.

One of the common myths about Trusts is that they are complex and difficult to administer. Competent counsel can assist you to understand the ease in which a Trust can be administered and the elimination of some of the costs and delays which might otherwise occur.

PRUDENT MAN

Q. *What is the "Prudent Man Rule" as pertaining to Trustees?*

A. Trustees are subject to the "Prudent Man Rule" and have been for a long time. The rule can generally be defined as one requiring the Trustee to preserve capital and avoid risk. The Trustee must make the Trust property productive but must not speculate in anything which could cause a loss of the capital assets.

The Trustee is accountable for all of the assets of the Trust and cannot offset losses from imprudent or speculative investments against gains otherwise achieved. The Trustee also has a duty to diversify the investments in a Trust in order to minimize the risk of losses. There is also a duty to dispose of investments which have become unsuitable for the Trust.

Assets in a Trust must be selected, at a minimum, with the skill and diligence of an "ordinary prudent individual." Trustees must also follow the terms of the Trust. Much has been written about the ordinary prudent individual. Such an individual must exercise judgment and care in selecting assets as well as using skill, prudence and diligence in maintaining them.

In deciding whether or not a Trustee has breached his duty as an ordinary prudent individual, all of the facts of each case must be decided. It should be obvious that a bank Trust department would have a much higher degree of duty as Trustee than an individual. It should also be obvious that a Trustee has a great deal of responsibility.

Persons who choose to have a Trust, should consider the above factors before deciding to have their Trust continue a long time after their death. If the Trust calls for "income only" for a number of years, it may be better to have a professional Trustee rather than an individual Trustee. If the Trust is to terminate upon death and be totally distributed at that time, then the person preparing the Trust can choose between a professional and a "prudent man."

ESTATE PLANNING

PROBATE DEFINITIONS

ESTATE PLANNING GOALS

Q. *What should I strive for in planning my estate?*

A. Everyone has different goals and different objectives in planning their estate. I believe everyone should be concerned about seven basic goals:

1. *Minimizing the cost of estate settlement.* This goal can be established in a variety of different ways including a Living Trust, joint ownership, "in Trust for" and creating life estates. Simple Wills by themselves *cannot* accomplish this goal.
2. *Minimizing the time of estate settlement.* Would you prefer your estate to go through a long delay caused by the court system or have it be distributed and administered very quickly? If you have all of your assets in your name and you have a simple Will you have guaranteed a long process before your estate can be closed.
3. *Minimizing the complexity of estate planning.* Estate settlements can be complex especially if the beneficiaries are not in agreement and there is a lack of direction given by the deceased. If you fail to make a Will or Trust, chaos could occur. The state of Florida has made a Will for you if you fail to make one yourself.
4. *Minimizing the total liability of the estate.* Estates can pass tax free $400,000 in 1985, $500,000 in 1986, and $600,000 in 1987. Larger estates can pass up to $1,200,000 estate tax free. Why pay tax when you don't have to? However, to accomplish maximum tax and probate savings, you must see a competent estate planning attorney.
5. *Maximizing the family's privacy.* Wills are a public document upon death, a copy of which anyone can purchase. Much of your estate can bypass your Will and the court system, thereby giving your family complete privacy in a time of sorrow.
6. *Providing adequate management and control during the lifetime and after the death of either or both spouses.* The use of a durable family power of attorney and careful selection of Trustees of your Trust can provide the best management control and guardianship planning.
7. *Minimizing the likelihood of contests during estate settlement.* Most Will contests occur because of poor planning. The use of video equipment is becoming a popular way for persons to explain why they have planned their estate to treat beneficiaries unequally or to omit them altogether.

Failure to plan any of the above can lead to economic waste of your estate. Don't delay in making these important decisions.

FRAUD IN ESTATE PLANNING

Q. *Can a person be guilty of fraud in any phase of estate planning?*

A. Yes. If a transfer of an asset was made as part of an estate plan and it was intended to defraud creditors at the time of transfer, it can be considered as fraud. In order to prove fraud it is usually necessary to prove several of the following, "badges of fraud":

1. Insolvency or indebtedness of the debtor;
2. Transfer of the debtor's entire estate;
3. Special relationship between transferor and transferee;
4. Conveyance of property that lacked any consideration;
5. Conveyance of assets but reservation of benefits to the debtor;
6. Concealment or secrecy of the conveyance or transfer of the assets;
7. Pending threat of litigation against the debtor.

It is the writer's opinion that the most important of the eight points listed above is the threat of litigation. Lack of a threat of litigation could easily allow one to plan their estate in any way they choose.

There are many categories of property that are not subject to the claims of creditors as to a forced sale of property. Some of them are as follows:

a. Homestead exemption—1/2 acre of a municipal homestead or up to 160 acres of non-municipal homestead are exempt from execution.
b. Personal property exemption which includes $1,000.00 of personal items are exempt from execution.
c. Wages or earnings for personal labor or services are exempt from execution as according to Florida Statute 222.11-12.
d. Pensions, annuities and retirements under Florida Retirement System and State and County Retirement Systems, and Teachers' Retirement System are exempt from execution.
e. Certain types of life insurance arrangements are exempt.
f. All disability income benefits are exempt unless effected to defraud creditors.
g. Workers compensation payments are exempt from execution.
h. Unemployment compensation payments are exempt from execution except for child support payments.
i. Fraternal Benefit Society payments are also exempt.

As you can tell, many factors are involved in your estate plan and competent counsel should be used to assist you.

ESTATE TAXES—FORM 706

Q. *What estates have to file a tax return?*

A. The Internal Revenue Code mandates that the "executor" of the estate of every citizen or resident of the United States must file an estate tax return if the total of the gross estate is valued at the date of death at (1)

1985—$400,000

1986—$500,000

1987—$600,000

plus (2) the taxable gifts made by the decedent after 1976 which are not included in the decedent's gross estate, plus (3) the amount of the specific $30,000 gift tax exemption allowed under the IRC #2521, with respect to gifts made after September 8, 1976, and before 1977.

Estates of citizens or residents dying before January 1, 1977, were required to file an estate tax return if the value of the gross estate on the date of decedent's death exceeded $60,000, even though the value of the gross estate was $60,000 or less on the alternate valuation date.

The Internal Revenue Code provides that the federal estate tax return must be filed within nine months after the date of the decedent's death unless an extension of time for filing the return has been granted.

Failure to file the federal estate tax entails a number of penalties. If the failure is a willful one, the person required to make the return is subject to fine and imprisonment. Normally, failure to file is not willful but attributed to delinquency and only a penalty is accessed.

The Estate Tax Form (706) is comprehensive and includes Schedules on 1) Real Estate; 2) Stocks and Bonds; 3) Mortgages, Notes and Cash; 4) Insurance; 5) Jointly Owned Property; 6) Miscellaneous Property; 7) Transfer During Decedent's Life; 8) Powers of Appointment; 9) Annuities; 10) Funeral Expenses; 11) Debts and Mortgages; 12) Losses; 13) Bequests; 14) Valuation; 15) Charitable Bequests; 16) Foreign Credits; 17) Tax Credits; 19) Computation Tax.

Many procedures can be implemented to reduce taxes and persons with taxable estates should seek accounting or legal advice in ways to reduce tax liability. A thorough discussion should also take place with a competent legal advisor concerning a reduction of administration expenses upon death.

Income taxes can also be dramatically reduced while you are living with the help of a competent advisor. Often a financial planner or accountant and an attorney can act as a team to take care of your financial, tax, and legal needs.

ESTATE EXPENSES

Q. *What order or priority do bills, debts, and other expenses have to be paid from an estate?*

A. There are seven classes of which the personal representative should pay the expenses of administration and claims against an estate:

CLASS I: Court costs and administrative costs as well as personal representative and attorney fees are the highest priority.

CLASS II: Reasonable funeral expenses, interment and grave marker expenses are the next priority. These expenses may be paid by the personal representative or guardian and should not exceed $1,500.00.

CLASS III: State and federal taxes and debts with preference under federal law should be paid as the priority.

CLASS IV: Medical and hospital expenses during the last 60 days of illness of the decedent. This class also includes the expenses of anyone taking care of the decedent.

CLASS V: Family Allowance: The decedents domiciled in Florida at the time of death could be allowed homestead and exempt property plus "family allowance." Family Allowance is an allowance permitted by the court after notice and a hearing, not exceeding a total of $6,000.00.

CLASS VI: This class pertains to debts acquired after death by the *continuation* of the decedent's business. The debts may not exceed the assets of the business.

CLASS VII: The last class considers all other claims including judgments or decrees.

If there is insufficient monies to pay the debts of any one class (listed above) the debts of all the preceding classes shall be paid and monies left over shall be prorated in the next class.

ESTATE PLANNING FOR WIDOWS

Q. *What advice can you give a widow concerning her financial and estate planning problems?*

A. Every widow has unique problems as well as many common ones. For example, a widow with children living close by has completely different problems than a widow with children living far away, or a widow without children.

One of the most important concerns facing widows is that of planning for incompetency. There are several planning techniques for this, including but not limited to, durable family power of attorney, Revocable Trust, and Irrevocable Trust. Guardianship costs can be expensive, and a careful plan can eliminate or reduce these costs dramatically.

Minimizing probate and administration costs may or may not be of concern. Widows with children are usually concerned about the high cost of probate while widows without children sometimes place a low priority on probate costs. Widows should remember that their last Will and testament will be probated unless they make special arrangements. Those special arrangements should be made with an attorney specializing in estate work with a desire to help his clients avoid probate.

Gifting can be reviewed in two ways as far as widows are concerned. Widows could be advised to exercise restraint in making gifts which would delete the estate cash needed for income and security or they could (with larger estates) be advised to maximize gifts to avoid income and estate taxation.

Prenuptial agreements would probably be advisable for widows planning re-marriage. Such agreements are helpful in solving after-death disputes between children and in solving problems which may arise if the marriage ends in divorce.

A widow should seek the advice of more than one professional regarding what her investment portfolio should consist of. Often tax-free securities are appropriate as a means to reducing income taxation, and financial planning can result in a higher monthly income at a lower tax rate.

In the way of non-legal advice, widows should join clubs and church groups and keep a variety of friends to socialize with. Also, a good relationship with an attorney is desirous when quick, legal information is needed, or action can be taken by an attorney who is familiar with the circumstances.

ESTATE PLANNING FOR BACHELORS

Q. *What should a bachelor be concerned with in planning his estate?*

A. Bachelors can do effective estate planning as well as other categories of people. In many cases brothers, sisters, nephews and nieces are the likely beneficiaries. Colleges and charities may also be favored by the bachelor.

The unlimited marital deduction which can be effectively used between husband and wife is not available to the bachelor, but sound tax strategies such as gifting and bequests to educational institutions and charities can be used. Often bachelors with large estates effectively use life insurance owned by the members of his family or a charity, with annual gifts from the bachelor to pay the premiums.

If the bachelor has minor nieces or nephews of a deceased brother or sister, he may want to set up Trusts that provide for their education, medical support and allow for standard of living provisions. Trusts are also effective ways for the bachelor to leave income (not principal) to parents, incompetent or disabled family members, for the duration of their lifetime, and then upon their death, to leave the principal to a particular institution, charity, or family member. Bachelors often set up educational foundations in their own name. The estate owner then can name the foundation as the residuary beneficiary of his estate which may provide a federal tax savings.

If the bachelor is an owner and operator of a successful business enterprise, the disposition of the business should be considered. Typically, a buy-out of the bachelor's business by a co-owner or key personnel may be appropriate. Arrangements may be made with key employees or other business acquaintances to purchase the business with a buy-sell agreement funded with life insurance.

The use of Trusts are very popular with bachelors. They often are not extremely close to other family members and do not want to burden others with the delays, costs, and situations which arise in probate court. Thus, they find the Living Trust an effective tool to plan their estate so that it can be distributed quickly, and efficiently upon their death.

Single persons such as bachelors also find the guardianship planning features of a Trust reassuring for their estate planning needs.

ESTATE PLANNING FOR MARRIED COUPLES

Q. *Do married couples who own everything jointly need to worry about estate planning?*

A. Yes. Everyone should be concerned about estate planning. The tax laws created the unlimited marital deduction in 1981, which alleviated many of the tax concerns for married couples upon the death of the first spouse to die. Now it is possible to give your spouse an unlimited amount of money during lifetime or upon death, tax free.

However, if a decedent dies with a Will or Trust which was executed before September, 1981, which expressly provided that the spouse receive the maximum amount of property qualifying for the marital deduction, that amount is deemed to be the *prior* maximum, not the *new* unlimited amount, unless the formula is amended after September, 1981, specifically referring to the new amount.

Married couples should not delay their estate planning until the first spouse dies because:

1. Both could die at the same time in a common accident.
2. One could become incompetent and the other one die.
3. Both could become incompetent within a very short period of one another.

4. After the death of the first spouse, the one surviving may not have or take the opportunity to adequately plan his or her estate.

If you are fortunate enough to be married, why not do your estate planning together as a team instead of leaving it for the surviving spouse to worry over? Married couples often have durable family powers of attorney for one another which is an excellent tool if one becomes incompetent or incapable of signing checks, stock certificates or other financial instruments. Powers of attorney are not effective upon death or when one becomes adjudicated incompetent.

Estate planning for children is important for married couples. Most parents will leave everything to their children outright upon death. However, some parents will choose to spread out payments to their children over a number of years to prevent the children from spending the entire estate very quickly.

Joint ownership of assets or individual ownership of assets should be carefully considered for married couples. Often second marriages result in individual ownership of assets, and couples with assets over $600,000.00 should discuss the advisability of separating their assets.

Married couples should also explore the advantages of Trusts in their estate planning to avoid probate, plan guardianship, insure privacy, and ease the administrative procedures and quickness of the distribution of the estate.

ESTATE PLANNING FOR CHILDREN

Q. *What are some of the estate planning techniques that I need to be concerned with in planning for my minor children?*

A. There are many different approaches to estate planning for children. One of the foremost concerns for any couple with minor children is that the children would be properly cared for in the event of a common disaster. Insurance is a common tool to provide enough money for the support of the children.

However, money is not enough to raise children, and the selection of a guardian for the children should be carefully considered. The responsibility of distributing the money to the guardian from either the estate or from insurance can be controlled through a Trust or through the Probate and Guardianship Court. The decision-making process of how the guardian would receive the monies to care for the children should be decided when the Will or Trust is drawn by the attorney.

The money for college education is another concern for estate planners and parents. Planning for college expenses is often accomplished with insurance, special saving accounts, annuities, or a variety of other financial planning tools. Usually an attorney and a financial advisor make an excellent team in planning for college expenditures.

As estate planning tool which is sometimes used by parents is to spread out payment to children over a period of time in order for the children not to receive their entire inheritance at an early age. For example, some parents might plan for their children to receive 50% of their inheritance at age 21 and 50% at the age of 25 or 30. This would avoid the mismanagement of an entire estate at once.

Planning for emergency medical costs is another very important aspect in planning for the care of children. Parents should properly plan their own disability insurance in order for the children's support to be continued in a time of illness or other incapacity. Often medical misfortunes of the parents or children can cause financial disaster to a family without proper insurance planning.

Another important element of estate planning for children is reducing or eliminating probate costs and arranging for the children to receive monies from the estate easily and quickly. This goal can be achieved often by the use of Inter Vivos or Living Trusts. A review of how this could be accomplished should be discussed with your attorney.

ESTATE PLANNING FOR DIVORCEES

Q. *What estate planning techniques are important for divorcees?*

A. I will assume, for the purpose of this question, that the divorced person has not remarried and has children from a prior marriage.

Many of the considerations regarding the children may or may not be covered in the Final Divorce Judgment. For example, medical and dental insurance, term or health insurance may also be required by the court to cover hospital or medical expenses and to cover expenses and support money upon the death of one of the parents. In any case, proper planning should be implemented to provide for any education, medical needs and standard of living expenses for children.

One of the more important aspects of estate planning for divorcees is an immediate review of Wills or Trusts to eliminate provisions for a divorced spouse. In some cases, this may occur automatically, however, the documents should still be reviewed along with life insurance policies and deeds and titles to real and personal property.

The unlimited marital deduction is not available to divorced or single persons and an estate analysis may be necessary to determine what estate taxes may have to be paid. If estate taxes are a fact of life, the divorced person should consider life insurance as a possible means to cover the tax liability.

Minor children will dictate the necessity of guardianship planning in the event of an unexpected death. Proper estate and financial planning are also necessary to insure that enough monies are available to support the children until they reach majority age.

Divorcees should also be careful with estate planning if they are considering remarriage. Strong consideration should be given to a prenuptial agreement which would detail respective interests upon death or divorce in each spouse's estate. If each spouse has a separate estate, he or she may wish to plan to relinquish any interest in the estate of the other. In a second marriage, planning how husband and wife will hold their assets, who the beneficiaries of the assets are, and to what level they will support each other upon death, are crucial to estate planning for divorcees. As in all estate planning, one must decide if a Will is sufficient or whether a Trust should be used in one's estate plan.

ESTATE PLANNING FOR LARGE ESTATES

Q. *What estate planning techniques are necessary for large estates?*

A. For purposes of your question, I will assume a large estate to be over $600,000.00 Tax-law changes allow $600,000.00 to be given away estate-tax-free in 1987. For purposes of explanation I will call the above amount the "exempt amount." With careful planning, using a separation of estates between husband and wife, up to $1,200,000.00 can be left estate-tax-free in 1987.

Trusts, both revocable and irrevocable, are often used in estate planning for large estates to avoid probate and shorten the administration process. However, Trusts are effective in all types of estates, large and small, and should not be considered as tools only for large estates.

Another popular planning tool in large estates is gifting. Gifting can help especially when an asset such as land is expected to appreciate substantially in the future, thereby increasing the size of the estate even greater. Gifting can also be used to memorialize the donor to a charity or allow children to carry on a business. As gifts are made, the size of the large taxable estate is reduced, and probate and administrative costs are eliminated from the items that are given away.

Using a qualified pension plan is another excellent method to avoid estate taxation on at least part of the estate and preserving the benefits of enjoyment for the entire family. Monies left through a qualified pension plan may avoid estate tax up to $100,000.00.

Another means of reducing or, in some cases, eliminating estate tax is through the installment sale technique. Installment sales freeze the value of the asset (land or business) at today's price and will prevent assets from appreciating higher, which otherwise would have caused a higher appraisal of the estate— thus higher taxes. Installment sales are also a method to pass property to heirs earlier than they would have received them, and at the same time provide additional cash income to the sellers.

Estate planning for a large estate requires a full understanding of the assets in the estate and an overall plan of how the estate would be protected and managed in order to avoid taxation.

ESTATE PLANNING FOR BUSINESS OWNERS

Q. *What should a business owner be concerned with in estate planning?*

A. One of the major concerns that business owners should have in estate planning is the continuation of the business after death. If the business is a sole proprietorship, the business would have to go through a probate procedure and court approval would be necessary for the continuation of the business. This procedure would include (1) a petition to the court requesting that the business be continued and stating the reasons why; (2) listing a schedule of the assets of the business; and (3) the period of time in which the business is to continue.

The order from the court would state (1) the period of time in which the business is to continue; and (2) the powers that the personal representative has in the continuation of the business; and (3) the form and nature of the accounting required by the business.

It should be obvious that if a business is to be continued through the probate process, it can be a long, time-consuming and costly process.

Other types of businesses, such as a corporation, may continue without a court order, but often the corporate stock of the decedent may have to go through the probate process.

Partnership agreements will generally have provisions as to what happens upon the death of a partner as to the ownership and continuation of a business. Buy-sell agreements should be considered by business owners in order to plan for the death of a partner. These agreements, if funded by insurance, provide for critical dollars with which to continue a business upon the death of a key person. Key-man insurance is also a very important element for the continuance of a business and often provides funds for interim periods until other key persons can be found.

There has been an emergence of the "Business Trust" which an owner of a business sets up so that upon the death of the business owner, the business can be run by a committee which bypasses the probate process. Business property can also be placed into a Trust to avoid probate.

There are numerous ways for a business owner to freeze his interest in a corporation and let the shares owned by family members grow. This method may reduce the taxation of the senior business member's estate. Partnership interests can also be frozen as a means to reduce federal estate taxation.

ESTATE PLANNING FOR PETS

Q. *What planning techniques should I consider in estate planning for my pet?*

A. Pet owners often forget or purposefully do not plan for their pet in the event their pet should outlive them. If your pet is important to you and you have a plan for it after your death, you should consider the following:

1. Make a disposition of the pet in your Will or Trust to a relative or friend. After the pet is given to them it becomes their property and they are free to do with it as they see fit.
2. You may also give instructions as to the disposition of your pet in your "Separate Writing" or "Letter of Instruction" authorized by your Will.
3. If you wish your pet to be put to "sleep" upon your death, you should leave the appropriate instructions with your personal representative or other family members.
4. If you wish to leave part of your estate for the maintenance and care of your pet for the life of the pet, you should consider the use of a Trust to eliminate court fees and probate cost for this type of activity. Provisions for the remainder of any monies after the pets death should also be made.

It is not uncommon for pet lovers who have no children to leave their entire estates to the SPCA or other concerns such as the Seabird Sanctuary. This type of giving can also offer certain types of tax advantages to larger estates.

Few people plan for disabilities resulting in their being unable to take care of themselves and their pet. In many cases the use of a Living Trust can provide a guardianship plan for themselves and their pet without having to use the guardianship court. This type of planning can eliminate attorney fees and court costs. The selection of a Trustee to take over upon death or incapacity is critical to successful planning of this type.

If upon the death of a pet owner, the disposition of a pet has not been planned and no one steps forward to provide for the pet, it is usually taken to the county facility for animals where it will be sheltered for a few days and if no one wants it, the pet will be put to "sleep." Planning for pets is often overlooked. What is going to be the fate of your pet? If you care and want to provide for your pet or leave instructions for its disposition, DO IT NOW.

ESTATE PLANNING FOR THE HANDICAPPED

Q. *What estate planning techniques should be considered for the handi-capped?*

A. Many factors should be considered in planning and providing for handicapped persons. One of the most important elements in planning for a handicapped person who receives government benefits is the careful planning of the inheritance of property which may make him or her ineligible to receive those benefits. To accomplish this is not an easy matter, as it takes the careful planning of a competent estate-planning attorney.

A Trust is commonly used to provide for the needs of the handicapped, but is restrictive enough to prevent the beneficiary from unwisely spending the income and corpus. Language in a Trust can provide supplemental care and maintenance to government benefits. Such language in the Trust would normally begin, "The express purpose of this Trust is to provide for X's extra and supplemental care, maintenance, support and education in addition to and over and above the benefits received by X from state or federal agencies for his/her disability.

Guardianship planning is necessary for handicapped children who are living at home and are not under the care of a state or federal hospital or agency. Guardians should be chosen to control all real and personal property and to approve all financial aspects of the handicapped beneficiary's estate. This appointment is made when it is determined that the handicapped beneficiary does not have sufficient capacity to manage his property or financial affairs.

Retirement income and expenses for handicapped persons are important in planning one's estate. All planned sources of income should be totalled and then all expected expenses should be totalled. If the monthly expenses exceed the monthly income then additional planning steps are necessary.

Insurance is often a common way to plan for the care, maintenance and support of a handicapped person. There are four areas of consideration for life insurance in your financial plan:

1. Protection of beneficiaries including paying the cost of funeral and administrative expenses;
2. Estate tax considerations—under the 1981 tax law there is an unlimited marital deduction and $600,000.00 may be passed, tax free in 1987;
3. Changing value of life insurance—your policy should be reviewed at least every other year to see if it is sufficient for its purpose;
4. Income—as people get older, their need for insurance usually lessens, although this may not be true in a "handicapped situation." An income analysis should be undertaken to determine if present insurance will provide enough future income.

ESTATE PLANNING/POST-MORTEM

Q. *What can I do now to make it easier on my children after my death?*

A. Assuming that your Will and/or Trust are in order and you have properly planned to eliminate or reduce estate taxes, a Letter of Instructions kept with your Will and/or Trust would be extremely helpful. The letter would cover some or all of the following:

1. The location of your important papers, including where the original Will and/or Trust may be kept;
2. An explanation of the assets and how they are to be used for the surviving spouse;
3. A listing of names, addresses and telephone numbers for reference, including accountant, attorney, broker, banks, relatives and friends;
4. As much information as possible about bank accounts, CD's, checking accounts, safe deposit boxes, business affairs, and other contracts;
5. A list of life insurance policies and company pension benefits and who to contact concerning these;
6. The location of separation or divorce agreements as well as birth certificates, adoption information and the like;
7. The location of income, gift, and other tax returns, and any information necessary regarding tax returns and forms to be filed;
8. A list of credit cards and all other credit arrangements so that such arrangements can be immediately cancelled or changed;
9. Instructions as to club memberships, dues paid annually, and to whom club files and records should be returned;
10. A list of the addresses and telephone numbers of all the beneficiaries;

In addition to the above information, many Florida Wills authorize a "Separate Writing." A Separate Writing is an itemized list of personal effects such as clothing, jewelry, furniture, etc. which you desire to be passed to a particular person. For example, a woman may wish for her oldest daughter to receive all of her jewelry; or if she has several daughters, she can itemize certain pieces for each daughter. A father may wish his oldest son to have a gun collection, coin collection, or other heirlooms passed from generation to generation. These types of items can be effectively passed down the family line through a "Separate Writing" and included with your Will.

Great care should be taken to avoid conflict, disagreements and disputes at the time of death. Often, controversy begins over very small items and then the beneficiaries find they cannot agree on anything.

Wills, Trusts, Letters of Instructions, and Separate Writings should be reviewed at least every two years and sometimes even annually depending on the circumstances. The tax laws changed dramatically in 1981, and anyone with a Will or Trust which refers to a prior tax act should have their Will or Trust reviewed.

LIFETIME GIFTS

Q. *What are the advantages and disadvantages of "lifetime gifts"?*

A. "Lifetime Gifts" are a method to reduce income and estate tax. There is no tax on gifts given to spouses during life or upon death and $10,000 may be given to any other person without a tax. The "giver" has to pay a tax on all amounts over $10,000. In order for a gift to be bona fide or a valid gift, it must meet the following criteria:

1. The donor must be competent and understand the nature of the gift.
2. The donee must be capable of receiving the gift.
3. There must be a clear and unmistakable intention on the part of the donor to absolutely and irrevocably divest himself of the title, dominion, and control of the subject matter.
4. There must be an irrevocable transfer of the present legal title and of the control of the entire gift to the donee, in order for the donor to be unable to exercise further dominion or control over it.
5. Delivery to the donee of the gift.
6. Acceptance of the gift.

It should be noted that to further qualify for a gift, the property must be given without any consideration.

The main reason for establishing the gift tax is to prevent people from avoiding the progressive federal estate tax by gifting their assets while they are living.

CHARITABLE GIFTS: A deduction is allowable on the federal gift tax return for certain gifts to qualified charities. Gifts made to religious, charitable, scientific, literary, and educational organizations are generally deductible.

DISADVANTAGES OF LIFETIME GIFTS:

1. Making taxable gifts results in prepayment of tax.
2. Lifetime taxable gifts increase the unified transfer tax rate effective at death.
3. Some gifts made within three years of death are included within the gross estate.
4. If taxable gifts are made, there is a reduction in the amount of the unified credit available at death.

ADVANTAGES OF LIFETIME GIFTS:

1. Eliminates some appreciation from the estate.
2. Allows donor to transfer income-producing property to beneficiaries who may be in low-income tax brackets.
3. Lifetime gifts of up to $10,000 per donee, per year, ($20,000 for married couples), are tax exempt transfers.

4. Gifts made in contemplation of death are not grossed-up in the donor's estate.

Gifting is only one element of estate planning. Consult your attorney before you take action.

PROBATE DEFINITIONS

"AUTHENTICATED" when referring to copies of documents or judicial proceedings required to be filed with the court shall mean a certified or a copy authenticated according to s.1738 or 2741, Title 28, U.S.C.

"BENEFICIARY" means heir-at-law in an intestate estate; devisee in a testate estate; and the owner of a beneficial interest in a Trust. The term does not apply to an heir-at-law, devisee or owner of a beneficial interest in a Trust after his interest in the estate or Trust has been satisfied.

"CERTIFIED COPY" means a copy of a document signed and verified as a true copy by the officer to whose custody the original is entrusted.

"CLAIMS" means liabilities of the decedent, whether arising in contract, in tort, or otherwise, and funeral expenses. The term does not include expenses of administration, estate, inheritance, succession or other death taxes.

"CLERK" means the clerk or deputy clerk of the court.

"CODE" means the Florida Probate Code as amended from time to time.

"COURT" means the Circuit Court.

"CURATOR" means a person appointed by the Court to take charge of the estate of a decedent until letters are issued.

"DEVISE" when used as a noun, means a testamentary disposition of real or personal property and when used as a verb means to dispose of real or personal property by Will. The terms includes "gift", "give", "bequeath", and "legacy".

"DEVISEE" means a person designated in a Will to receive a devise. In the case of a devise to an existing Trust or Trustee, or to a Trustee or a Trust described by Will, the Trust or Trustee is the devisee. The beneficiaries of the Trust are not devisees.

"DISTRIBUTEE" means a person who has received estate property from a personal representative other than as a creditor or purchaser. A Testamentary Trustee is a distributee only to the extent of distributed assets or increments to

them remaining in his hands. A beneficiary of a Testamentary Trust to whom the Trustee has distributed property received from a personal representative is a distributee. For purposes of this provision, "Testamentary Trustee" includes a Trustee to whom assets are transferred by Will, to the extent of the devised assets.

"DOMICILE" shall be a person's usual place of dwelling and shall be synonymous with "residence".

"ESTATE" means property of a decedent that is the subject of administration.

"FILE" means to file with the court or the clerk.

"FOREIGN PERSONAL REPRESENTATIVE" means a personal representative of another state or foreign country.

"FORMAL NOTICE" means notice as required under Probate & Guardianship Rule 5.040 (a).

"FPC" means the Florida Probate Code, as amended from time to time.

"HEIRS" or *"HEIRS-AT-LAW"* means those persons, including the surviving spouse, who are entitled under the statutes of intestate succession to the property of a decedent.

"INCOMPETENT" means a minor or a person adjudicated incompetent.

"INFORMAL NOTICE" means notice as required under Probate & Guardianship Rule 5.040 (b).

"INTERESTED PERSON" means any person who may reasonably be expected to be affected by the outcome of the particular proceeding involved. In any proceeding affecting the estate, or the rights of a beneficiary in the estate, the personal representative shall be deemed to be an interested person. The term does not include an heir-at-law or devisee who has received his distribution. The meaning as it relates to particular persons may vary from time to time and must be determined according to the particular purpose of, and matter involved in, any proceeding.

"JUDGE" means the judge of the circuit court, including any judge elected, appointed, substituted or assigned to serve as judge of the court.

"LETTERS" means authority granted by the court to the personal representative to act on behalf of the estate of the decedent and as used in the Rules refers to what has been known as letters testamentary and letters of administration. All letters shall be designated "Letters of Administration".

"OTHER STATE" means any state of the United States other than Florida and includes the District of Columbia, The Commonwealth of Puerto Rico, and any territory or possession subject to the legislative authority of the United States.

"PERSONAL REPRESENTATIVE" means the fiduciary appointed by the court to administer the estate, and includes what has been known as an adminis-

trator, administrator cum testamento anexo, administrator de bonis non, ancillary administrator, ancillary executor, or executor to whom letters of administration have been issued.

"PETITION" means a written request to the court for an order.

"PROPERTY" means both real and personal property or any interest in it and anything that may be the subject of ownership.

"RESIDENCE" shall be a person's usual place of dwelling and shall be synonymous with "domicile".

"TRUSTEE" includes an original, additional, surviving, or Successor Trustee, whether or not appointed or confirmed by court.

"WILL" includes a codicil and is an instrument executed by a person in the manner prescribed by the Code and disposing of his property on or after his death including merely appointing a personal representative or revoking or revising another Will.

FAMILY/DIVORCE

BECOMING ADULTS

Q. *At what age are children responsible for their own debts?*

A. Generally, parents are responsible for their children until their 18th birthday. Some exceptions to this rule are as follows:

1. Minors who are married may assume the management of their estate, make contracts, sue and be sued and perform all other acts that an adult could.
2. Minors who have reached the age of 16 may borrow money for their own higher educational expenses. Such minors can sign promissory notes, contracts, and have the same effect as if they were an adult.
3. Minors who have reached the age of 17 may give consent to the donation of blood. Parents, however, may object in writing to said donation.
4. Under certain conditions, emergency medical care or treatment may be given to minors without parental consent. Generally this would occur if the delay of emergency medical care would have endangered the health of the minor. Physicians, hospitals or college health services shall not incur civil liability by reason of having rendered emergency medical care.
5. Unmarried pregnant minors may consent to the performance of medical or surgical care or services relating to their pregnancy.
6. Minors may be adjudicated as an adult and may be turned over to the supervision of the Department of Corrections under certain conditions.
7. In some cases, a parent's obligation to support children with physical deficiencies or mental deficiencies will continue past the age of 18.
8. Parents cannot usually be forced to pay for a child's college education. However, a husband or wife can certainly agree as part of a property settlement, that one party will pay for education of their child through college or beyond.

DIVORCE

Q. *I just moved to Florida and want to divorce my husband. What do you suggest I do?*

A. Move back to the state where you came from. Florida has a six months residence requirement before you can even file for a divorce. If you can wait six months, the divorce procedure is fairly simple, if your marriage is irretrievably broken.

Q. *I just left my husband. We are not desirous of a court battle over our property. Can a settlement be made to avoid a court battle?*

A. Yes. A property and separation agreement can be written if both parties agree and if husband and wife can agree on property distribution, alimony, child support, custody, and visitation rights. Such agreements should be reviewed by attorneys representing each party as the attorney drafting the agreement can only represent one party. All signatures on the document should be notarized.

Q. *I recently moved to Florida and need advice regarding divorce. My wife and I own extensive properties in Virginia. My wife is very much against the divorce and refuses to sign any agreements. Will Florida courts divide the property in Virginia if one party still lives in Virginia?*

A. No. The Florida courts will grant a divorce if one party has lived in Florida for six months, but will not generally make property settlement agreements on out-of-state property under the above circumstances.

Q. *What does a divorce cost?*

A. I presume your question refers to court costs, filing fees, and attorney fees. The present filing fee is $69.50 and the service of summons fee is $12.00 in Pinellas County. Final court costs vary depending on the circumstances, but are generally less than $75.00.

The attorney fees vary and it depends upon whether a property settlement agreement is drafted, how many meetings are necessary, if the matter is contested or uncontested, and how complicated the division of assets. Your attorney should disclose the fees before the case is accepted.

Q. *My divorce papers do not indicate who should receive the tax exemption for the children each year. The IRS just sent a letter that states both husband and wife have claimed the exemption. What should I do?*

A. If no provision is indicated on any agreement between husband and wife, the IRS will grant the exemption to the party which provides the greatest share of support to the children.

Q. *How long does the divorce procedure take?*

A. Under a non-emergency situation, the petitioner (person seeking the divorce) will have papers served on the respondent (other party). Once the papers have been served the respondent has 20 days to file the original of the denial with the clerk of the court or the petitioner's attorney. If the respondent fails to do so, a default will be entered against the respondent for the relief demanded in the petition.

Comment: This article should not be construed in any manner to encourage divorce. The writer personally encourages all parties having marital difficulties to seek help from qualified marriage counselors, psychologists or clergymen before seeking an attorney.

INVALID MARRIAGE

Q. *Can marriages be annulled in Florida?*

A. Yes. A marriage may be annulled for several reasons. There may have been a lack of legal or mental capacity to contract, or because of physical incapacities or infirmities or because of lack of content entering into the marriage. If a marriage was wrongfully procured by force, duress, fraud or concealment, it may also be invalid.

UNDESOLVED PRIOR MARRIAGE

In Florida, second marriages are not valid where the first marriage was never dissolved. If one were to conceal the fact of such a marriage, it may authorize an annulment on the grounds of fraud.

INCESTUOUS MARRIAGE

Marriages may be annulled if they are between brother and sister, aunt and nephew, uncle and niece or any parties related by "lineal consanquinity" (blood relationship).

NONAGE

Marriages cannot generally be annulled because one may be below the age of consent. This matter lies strictly in the discretion of the court and the marriage will be considered valid unless otherwise overturned.

MENTAL INCOMPETENCY

An absolutely essential element for an uncontested marriage is having sufficient mental capacity to agree or consent to the creation of the marital status. If the lack of mental capacity was temporary, it may still be sufficient to have the marriage annulled. If a person was "drugged" at the ceremony and not aware of his/her actions, the marriage may be annulled.

INTOXICATION

A marriage may be annulled if one of the parties was so intoxicated as to be unaware of what he/she was doing at the time of the ceremony. If the party was only slightly intoxicated, the decision would be one for the court to decide.

IMPOTENCY

Florida cases are somewhat vague as to whether impotency is grounds for an annullment. The indications are that impotency (inability to engage in, or a lack of capacity for normal, sexual intercourse) are sufficient grounds for annullment. Concealment of a disease is not grounds for annullment in the State of Florida.

MARRIAGE IN JEST

If a couple marries and one of the parties never intended to live with the other, cohabit or have sexual relations, the marriage will probably be considered not a true marriage and may be annulled.

DURESS

If the marriage was induced by force, restraint, threats, or duress of any type, then it may be annulled. The overpowering influence or threats of force must continue to the time of the marriage ceremony.

FRAUD OR CONCEALMENT

If an element of fraud is discovered that is deemed to be vital to the marriage relationship, it will probably be sufficient to have the marriage annulled. Concealment or misrepresentation as to a prospective spouse's marital status or premarital unchastity or parenthood may be grounds for annullment.

ANTENUPTIAL AGREEMENTS

Q. *My first marriage ended in a bitter divorce. I'm considering getting married again and would like to know how to protect myself.*

A. Antenuptial Agreements are very common especially when one of the parties is getting married for a second time. Such agreements provide for and are binding at time of dissolution or separation of marriage. The antenuptial agreement can actually serve as the separation and property settlement agreement at the time of a divorce.

Some of the standard features of such an agreement are:

(a) One party has assets that he or she would like to exclude from the new spouse's inheritance or protect from possible alimony.

(b) One spouse has business interests which he or she would like to protect from the other in time of death, separation or divorce.

(c) Each party would like to have separate financial accounts or own separate properties.

(d) In the event of dissolution of marriage, neither party would make claim for support or alimony upon the other party.

(e) Each party waives the right of statutory share, dower, any right of elective share to homestead, exempt property, family allowance, in and to the estate of the other and agree to make no claim of inheritance, descent, dower, curtesy, homestead, maintenance or statutory share of the estate of the other.

(f) Each agrees to pay all of their own expenses prior to the wedding.

(g) Each party does consent and acknowledge that the estate of the other party shall descend or be disposed of by Will to the heirs or legatees or devisees of each of said parties, free and clear of any claim by inheritance, dower, curtesy, maintenance statutory right and other claim by husband or wife.

(h) Each realizes that he or she is giving up certain rights established by law, and that such rights might well constitute a detriment and each is willing to assume said detriment with full knowledge and understanding thereof.

Summary: Antenuptial agreements are a very effective method of avoiding arguments, indecision, disagreements or disputes at time of death or divorce and serves as a binding agreement which will control the division of property or assets per the signed agreement.

JOINT OWNERSHIP

Q. *What are the major advantages and disadvantages of joint ownership?*

A. First of all, it is absolutely essential that you understand that joint ownership is not the answer for careful estate planning. For example, Fred and Mary jointly own 10,000 shares of AT&T stock valued at $70,000.00. This represents their major life savings with very little other liquid assets available. Fred has a monthly pension and social security check which provides nicely for their routine expenses. One day the unexpected happens—Fred has a major stroke. He is left paralyzed and mentally incompetent.

Q. *Can Mary cash in the stock?*

A. No. It is *jointly* held and requires both signatures.

Q. *What does Mary do now?*

A. Mary has to get her family attorney to petition the court to allow her to be appointed Guardian and Trustee of Fred's property. Although this is not a difficult task, it is a public one. In other words, the court proceeding that finds Fred incompetent to handle his own affairs is open to the public.

Q. *Can the judge appoint someone other than Mary as Trustee?*

A. Yes. Mary may have never before handled any financial affairs and be totally unfamiliar with taking care of such matters. The judge may appoint someone other than Mary to handle all financial affairs.

In the above example, neither joint ownership nor a common Will would have helped very much. The normal advantage of joint ownership is that the surviving half retains full ownership. In this case, Fred did not die but did become incompetent.

Although it is impossible to forecast what will happen in one's future, the above situation could have been averted if Fred and Mary had established a Living Trust.

- The Trust would have had a provision automatically making Mary Trustee and even appointing a successor if Mary became incompetent.
- It would have had a provision to use the appropriate funds to provide for Fred in his own home if practical.
- There would be no need for a court appearance as a Living Trust is a completely private matter.
- The stock could have been immediately cashed in, allowing for quick access to funds.

[NOTE] Living Trusts are not recommended in all cases. Consult your attorney for advice in this matter.

CHILD CUSTODY

Q. *Please discuss some of the legal ramifications and important considerations in recent child custody cases.*

1. *COURT DISCRETION*
   The court has broad discretion when awarding custody in the *final* decree but its decision is always subject to review as circumstances involving parents or guardians are recognized to be constantly changing.
2. *EFFECT OF DIVORCE*
   If the natural guardians of the child (mother & father) are divorced, the parent to whom custody of the child is awarded will be considered the guardian. When joint custody is awarded, both parents will continue as natural guardians. However, if custody is given to a non-parent, then both parents lose their status as natural guardian.
3. *JURISDICTION*
   The child must be residing in the area where the court has jurisdiction at the time the action is filed or the court will be considered not to have jurisdiction in the matter.
4. *AGREEMENTS TO CUSTODY*
   If the parties are able by agreement to work out a settlement concerning child custody, the courts will normally accept it. However, the court does have the power to reject the agreement if it is deemed not to be in the best interest of the child.

5. *WELFARE OF CHILD*

   The Dissolution of Marriage Act of 1971 provides that custody and visitation rights will be awarded in accordance with the best interests of the child. Therefore, the character and moral conduct of the person seeking custody will be probed and investigated. The type of home the child is to live in will also be ascertained.

6. *FINANCIAL CIRCUMSTANCES OF PARTIES*

   Financial considerations in Florida have never been the controlling factor in determining child custody. As long as one of the parents is able to provide the necessities of life and prevent welfare or costs to the community, the court can deem them as a capable parent.

7. *DIVIDED CUSTODY*

   Generally, if the child is very young, the court will award custody to one parent with reasonable visitation to the other. The primary objective of the court is to provide security and love for the child and not cause confusion as to where the child's home is situated.

8. *SEPARATION OF CHILDREN*

   Children in a family are normally kept together. Only for the most compelling reason, will children be divided.

9. *FITNESS OF PARENT*

   The court will hear testimony as to the unfitness of a parent. Generally the grounds where "unfitness" has been proven are:

   (a) Irresponsibility as a parent;   (b) Mental condition;

   (c) Constant use of drugs or alcohol;   (d) Marital misconduct.

   Adultery does not by itself necessarily prove that a parent is unfit to have custody. The court will examine the evidence (if presented) of the adverse effect, if any, the adultery has had on the child.

10. *PREFERENCE OF CHILD*

   A child's choice can be a factor in determining custody if the child is of sufficient age and intelligence and deemed by the court able to make a decision. The court will determine if one of the parents "poisoned" the mind of the child to influence a decision.

ADOPTION

Q. *Who can petition to adopt a child in Florida?*

A. A married couple, an unmarried adult, or either the husband or wife if the other spouse is a natural parent of the minor child may petition the Circuit Court of the county in which they reside to adopt the child.

Q. *Who gives consent for an adoption to take place in Florida?*

A. Consent may be executed by the court but normally consent has to be executed by:

    A. The mother of the minor;

    B. The father of the minor, if:

        (1) The minor was conceived or born while the father was married to the mother;

        (2) The minor is his child by adoption;

        (3) The minor has been established by court proceedings to be his child;

        (4) He has acknowledged in writing, signed in the presence of a competent witness, that he is the father of the minor child and has filed such acknowledgment with the Vital Statistics Office of the Department of Health and Rehabilitative Services.

    C. The minor, if more than 12 years or age, unless the court, in the best interest of the minor, disregards the minor's consent.

Q. *What are some of the procedures for a Florida adoption?*

A. Before a petition can be filed, the child must have lived in the home of the petitioner, except where:

    1. One of the petitioners is related to the child by blood or;

    2. The petitioners are related to the child as stepparents.

B. Notice of the final hearing on the adoption must be sent to the agency investigating the adoption and the Department of Health and Rehabilitative Services when its recommendation is required.

Stepparent adoptions no longer require such notices.

Q. *Is citizenship affected by adoption?*

A. No. Citizenship of an adopted child is not affected by his or her adoption, but naturalization of an adopted child is possible.

Q. *Are court records protected in an adoption proceeding?*

A. Yes. All records pertaining to the adoption are closed and kept in separate locked files. No person shall have access to these reports or records except upon court order.

Q. *What rights does the natural parent have after an adoption?*

A. The relationship of parent and child between the adopted person and his or her natural parents is completely altered and all the rights, duties and legal consequences cease to exist.

GIFTS TO MINORS

Q. *What are the legal and tax ramifications to making "gifts to minors"?*

A. Generally speaking, when you make a gift and set up an account to a minor it is irrevocable. In other words, the money belongs to the child as well as all the income derived therefrom. If the money is ever used for "paternal obligations," then the child could possibly have recourse against the parents for using or spending the money.

If the money has been set up in an account where the main objective is to shift income away from the parents to the children and the parents continue to use the money, the Internal Revenue could pursue serious charges of tax evasion.

"Gifts to minors" can be a very effective tool for shifting family income for college purposes or reducing the parents' taxable income. However, if this tactic is used, the game must be played as it was intended.

If the income from the "minor's" account is more than the minimum requirements established by the Internal Revenue Service, then a tax return will be necessary.

Another requirement of the "Gift to Minor" Act is that when the child reaches majority age the parent custodian has to turn over the account to the child.

An entirely separate matter is gifts to children who are not minors but are made to avoid inheritance or estate tax. The 1982 Tax Act allows for gifts to be made up to $10,000 per person tax free. Amounts over $10,000 are taxable.

Transferring money to children is not always a wise thing to do as complete control of the assets is lost and transferring may be subject to estate tax.

ALIMONY

Q. *Explain the difference between permanent alimony and rehabilitative alimony.*

A. The courts have determined that rehabilitative alimony is appropriate in situations where it is possible for a person to develop a new or redevelop a capacity for self-support and should be limited in amount and duration to what is necessary to maintain that person through his/her training or education or until he/she obtains employment or otherwise becomes self-supporting.

The considerations for rehabilitative alimony include age, education, duration of marriage, standard of living enjoyed during the marriage.

In cases where a spouse is a senior citizen and has never been employed, the court will usually award permanent alimony instead of rehabilitative alimony. In cases where a spouse has been accustomed to a high standard of living and has never been employed but has certain job skills thereby enabling him/her to reestablish himself/herself, then a mixture of both rehabilitative alimony and permanent alimony could be established.

Q. *What is the normal procedure regarding the marital home in divorce proceedings?*

A. There is no normal procedure regarding the marital home in divorce proceedings. The home may be sold with the equity being divided 50/50. The wife or husband may be allowed to live in the home for a certain number of years with the equity being divided when the house is finally sold. One party may receive the house as part of the separation agreement. There are many variables in deriving at who will retain possession or how the equity will be divided in a marital home during divorce proceedings.

Q. *What are the proper procedures to follow if a spouse stops making alimony payments?*

A. The court has provided a number of ways in which a spouse can collect alimony payments that have not been made. The methods include contempt proceedings, attachment proceedings, garnishment proceedings and a variety of other actions available to insure that alimony payments are met.

Q. *How difficult is it to modify a divorce agreement and judgment after the divorce?*

A. There are three areas that are generally subject to modification after a divorce. They are (1) modification of parental responsibility; (2) modification of alimony; (3) modification of child support. All three areas have definite procedures that can be followed to change judgments and agreements with appropriate cause. The courts will not hesitate to make changes in judgments or agreements if there is a sufficiency of pleadings to show just cause.

ELECTIVE SHARE AND HOMESTEAD RIGHTS

Q. *What effect does the elective share have on one's estate and how are homestead rights affected?*

A. In 1976, Florida abolished what was formerly known as "dower rights" which gave the widow/widower certain rights upon the death of a spouse. Dower rights were replaced with what is now known as elective share which states that the *surviving spouse* receives 30% of the decedent's personal and real property except for homestead property which is treated separately.

If the property (homestead) is owned jointly by husband and wife (tenancy by the entireties), it is not subject to the elective share as it will pass 100% to the surviving spouse.

In order to receive the elective share, the spouse must meet the following criteria:

- Spouse must file for the election (elective share) within four months of the decedent's death.
- In the event of litigation concerning the estate, the election period can be extended for 40 days.
- Elective shares cannot be assigned or transferred in any way as they are considered to be "personal rights."

If the decedent died without a Will and there is no election under elective share, the spouse will take property as outlined by the Florida Statutes.

If the decedent died with a Will and no election is made, the surviving spouse will take whatever the Will provides.

Homestead properties are deemed to be separate properties and are:

- Not subject to elective shares.
- Cannot be disposed of by Will except to surviving spouse, and then only if there are no minor children.
- Surviving spouse can in some circumstances obtain a life estate in the homestead with a vested remainder to the lineal descendants.
- Exempt from the execution of judgment liens (not including tax liens, vendor's liens, mechanic's liens, or mortgages).
- One-half acre within a municipality or 160 acres outside a municipality regardless of value.

Homesteads may be placed in a Living Trust under certain circumstances and probate may be avoided on the homestead but one should seek the advice of an attorney to avoid problems with the $25,000 real property deduction.

PROTECTING ASSETS FOR CHILDREN

Q. *How can I protect my assets for my children in regards to my husband's remarriage after my death or my remarriage after my husband's death?*

A. Your question must be answered in very general terms because there are many ways to approach a protection of assets for your children. Each method has pluses and minuses and only a few of the alternatives can be discussed here.

JOINT OWNERSHIP—Many people choose to own selected assets jointly with their children with the survivor having rights of ownership. Thus upon the death of the parent, the child would be the owner. Such an arrangement could be dangerous because the child (considered part owner) could be involved in a lawsuit or divorce or their assets could be subject to liability due to no fault of the parent. The child could also use the money against the wishes of the parent, and there is no guarantee that if the parent became incompetent that the money would be used in the parent's best interest.

"IN TRUST FOR"—This is a common approach that can be set up at most banks. Upon the death of the parent, the bank will release the money that it was "In Trust For." The difficulty with this arrangement is the complications upon incompetency, as the money does not pass until death. Other complications should be discussed with competent counsel.

PRENUPTIAL AGREEMENTS—In this arrangement the intended husband and wife agree before the marriage that each can keep assets in their own individual names and that those assets can pass free of any claim from the spouse. An agreement waiving any statutory rights to the deceased spouse's assets is signed and witnessed. The assets in this arrangement must be kept separate because if they become jointly owned by husband and wife, the prenuptial agreement may have a limited effect.

POSTNUPTIAL AGREEMENTS—A postnuptial agreement, with valid consideration, is an effective tool to use in protecting assets for children. Assets must be kept separate to be effective and the agreement must include a waiver of statutory rights.

LIVING TRUSTS—Many persons have turned to a Living Trust, keeping assets in their own Trust, leaving the income (only) to their spouse for life, and upon the death of the spouse, then the assets would go to their children. Such an arrangement keeps assets separate, avoids probate, and protects the children's assets while providing for one's spouse. Trusts can also offer tax advantages. Living Trusts can also be coupled with a prenuptial or postnuptial agreement. Trusts also give some "guardianship protection."

IRREVOCABLE TRUSTS—Irrevocable Trusts are much more restrictive as a way to protect assets for children and are not used as frequently as Living Trusts. Careful planning with competent counsel is necessary with this type arrangement.

SUMMARY—**Assets can be protected for children with careful planning. Waiting too late or delaying decisions greatly jeopardizes the outcome you may desire.**

GRANDPARENTS VISITATION

Q. *What rights do grandparents have to visit grandchildren once a divorce has taken place?*

A. Grandparents now have expanded visitation rights with minor grandchildren. Under a new Florida statute, the court may in its discretion award reasonable rights of visitation. The process is commenced by filing a petition and notice of filing with the Circuit Court by the grandparents. The notice and a copy of the petition are served on the parents of the minor child. Visitation rights can be awarded under three circumstances.

1. When one or both of the parents are deceased;

2. The marriage has been dissolved; or

3. A parent has deserted a minor child.

It should be noted that if grandparent visitation rights have been established in a particular case and the natural parent remarries, the visitation rights will not terminate. Even if the stepparent adopts the child, the natural grandparents' rights will not be terminated.

In a situation where both natural parents have died, it is unclear who would receive service of the petition, since the statute states it shall be served on the natural parents. However, living grandparents have certain rights as to guardianship of minor children when both natural parents have died and probably will play a part in selecting the new guardian. This new statute does not provide for grandparent visitation for children who are placed for adoption.

There has been considerable debate as to whether parents have a right to privacy with the raising of minor children, free from the interference of grandparents. The court must consider the parents' rights versus the child's rights versus the grandparents' rights. The traditional family unit would favor the occasional influence of a grandparent, and a child being deprived of that right would suffer an injustice.

Parents who do not honor court orders which allow visitation rights for grandparents are guilty of contempt of court and if repeated violations take place, they could eventually be placed in jail.

There are presently 47 states that have some form of a grandparent right statute. In Florida, due to the newness of the statute, many facets of it have been untried and untested.

YOUTHFUL MARRIAGES
AND PATERNITY PROCEEDINGS

Q. *What are the laws concerning persons under the age of 18 getting married?*

A. If either of the parties is under 18 years of age but is at least 16 years of age, the county court judge or clerk of the circuit court shall issue a license only if written consent is obtained from the parents. The consent must be acknowledged before an officer authorized to take acknowledgements and administer oaths. The license may be issued if both parents are deceased or if the minors had been previously married.

A second exception to the under 18 rule grants a county court judge discretion to issue a license to any male or female upon application of both parents that they are the parents of a child, or if a pregnancy is verified by the written statement of a licensed physician.

In cases where the male party does not wish to admit that he is the father and also tries to avoid financial responsibility, the mother may bring proceedings in circuit court to determine paternity. If the court determines the male party to be the father of the child, it may order the father to pay the mother, her guardian, or such other person assuming responsibility for the child, such sums sufficient to pay reasonable attorney's fee, hospital or medical expenses, etc.

As a guideline, Florida Statute 742.041 suggests the following monthly contributions for child support regarding paternity cases:

A. From date of birth to 6th birthday—$40.00 per month;

B. 6th birthday to 12th birthday—$60.00 per month;

C. 12th birthday to 15th birthday—$90.00 per month;

D. 15th birthday to 18th birthday—$110.00 per month.

The statute goes on to say that amounts may be increased or reduced by the judge in his discretion depending on the circumstances and the ability of the defendant to pay.

Upon marriage by the parties, the child will be deemed legitimate and the case may be dismissed. If the child were to be later adopted, the natural father would be relieved of any further child support.

INJURIES, DISABILITY AND DEATH

SEAT BELT LAW

Q. *Does the new seat belt law apply to old vehicles?*

A. First, here is a summary of how the new law works:

1. All front seat occupants (driver and passengers) must wear seat belts.
2. The driver is responsible for all front seat passengers (age 16 years or younger) and can be fined. The other passengers (over age 16) would receive their own ticket.
3. The child restraint statute requires that every driver shall protect children under six years of age. Children three years of age and younger have to be in a separate carrier while children four through five years of age have to be in a carrier or seat belt. Children six years of age or older have to wear a seat belt.

Some exemptions of the law are as follows:

1. You may be exempt if a licensed physician certifies that a seat belt should not be worn because of a medical condition.
2. Also some of the older cars are exempt such as:
   a. Cars manufactured before 1968;
   b. Trucks manufactured before 1972;
   c. School buses, public buses, farm equipment, motorcycles, mopeds, bicycles;
   d. Trucks in excess of 5,000 pounds.

It should be noted that Florida has established what is commonly referred to as the Seat Belt Defense Doctrine. Simply stated, the person causing an accident may argue that a person would have been injured to a lesser extent if that person had been wearing a seat belt. A classic example of this would be when a passenger is thrown through a windshield and suffers permanent facial scarring. The bottom line here is that your damage award may be reduced because you failed to wear your seat belt.

Statistics from other states that have adopted the "Seat Belt Law" show that deaths have dropped substantially. Now you have several reasons to "buckle up."

AUTOMOBILE ACCIDENTS

Q. *What should I do if involved in an automobile accident?*

A. You should follow the steps as outlined below:

1. *DON'T MOVE* Florida law requires you to stop at the scene. If you hit an unattended automobile you are required to leave a conspicuous note giving your name, address and vehicle registration number. You should also do what is possible so as not to impede traffic.

2. *HELP INJURED* Immediately determine if anyone is hurt and if so, seek the necessary assistance.

3. *PROTECT WHAT HAPPENED* Cars should not be removed unless they block or impede traffic. If they have to be moved, then careful notes should be taken as to the position of the cars at the time of impact. A drawing or sketch should be agreed upon by the drivers or with one driver and a non-interested witness.

4. *NOTIFY PROPER AUTHORITIES* A written report is required by Florida law for all accidents resulting in property damage of over $100.00. Police officers or sheriffs will furnish this report if they come to the accident scene, if not, you must provide the report.

5. *PROVIDE INFORMATION* Drivers are required to provide to each other their name, address and vehicle registration number. You are also required to provide to the investigating officer whatever information is needed to determine the cause of the accident. In addition, you will want to take your own notes, diagramming the scene, pacing off distances, noting skid marks, etc. You should also get the names and addresses of all witnesses and any statements made by them.

6. *MEDICAL ATTENTION* Even if you think your injury is not serious, you should see a doctor. This will help establish a "medical pattern" if you later have back or nerve damage, etc.

7. *NOTIFY YOUR INSURANCE COMPANY* Your insurance company should be notified immediately of the accident and you may wish your attorney to help you make a statement to them. Failure to make a prompt report could jeopardize your policy rights.

8. *INSURANCE PAYMENTS* Under Florida's no-fault insurance law, generally your own insurance company pays you 80% of your cost for medical care and treatment and 60% of lost income and your extraordinary expenses up to $10,000.00. Most drivers should also have comprehensive collision insurance as well as uninsured motorist protection.

9. *ATTORNEYS* Do not rush into a settlement. By carefully selecting an attorney you should maximize your results and protect your legal rights.

MOTOR VEHICLE NO-FAULT LAW

Q. *What are my rights under Florida's Motor Vehicle No-Fault Law?*

A. The Florida No-Fault Law is found in Florida Statute 627-730 through 627-7405. It can generally be said that its purpose is to provide for medical, surgical, funeral and disability insurance benefits without regard to fault. Some general statements concerning the law are as follows:

- Every owner or registrant of a motor vehicle is required to have insurance.
- Anyone failing to have insurance is personally liable for the damage he causes.
- The Department of Highway Safety and Motor Vehicles shall suspend the license of anyone operating a vehicle with inadequate insurance.

The No-Fault statute further requires that you have "PIP" or Personal Injury Protection insurance. This insurance would cover up to a limit of $10,000.00 for the loss sustained as a result of bodily injury, sickness, or disease arising out of injury. The payment would be as follows:

- 80% of all reasonable expenses for necessary medical, surgical, x-ray, dental and rehabilitative services.
- 60% of any loss of gross income and loss of earnings due to injuries sustained.
- Funeral, burial or cremation expenses up to $1,750.00 per individual.

Some of the standard exclusions allowed in policies are if the person caused damage to himself intentionally or if the damage was caused while committing a felony.

No-Fault coverage generally provides coverage to the insured, relatives in the same household, persons operating the insured motor vehicle, passengers in such motor vehicle, and other persons struck by the motor vehicle and suffering bodily injury. The No-Fault Law also provides methods for the insured or the attorney representing the insured to be assured of having firsthand proof of medical bills and records and statements concerning wages and earnings.

Further, anyone who obtains a drivers license by giving false information concerning insurance, through forgery or filing false proof, shall be guilty of a misdemeanor of the first degree. The punishment is as follows: Imprisonment of up to one year and a fine not to exceed $1,000.00.

UNINSURED MOTORIST

Q. *How can I protect myself against drivers who do not have insurance?*

A. You should immediately check your automobile insurance to see if *you* have purchased uninsured motorist coverage. This is an extra premium which you would pay to protect yourself from the improper driving of others. If you have purchased uninsured motorist insurance and are involved in an accident with an uninsured driver resulting in permanent your injuries, you would be entitled to damages from *your* insurance company. If you are involved in an accident with a driver who has limited liability insurance (such as $10,000.00) and your damages are greater than that amount, your uninsured motorist insurance may be responsible for the excess up to your policy limit.

Insurance companies are required to offer this insurance to you, but you do not have to accept it. Most professionals would advise you to definitely pay the extra premium for uninsured motorist insurance. You can easily check the declaration page of your policy to see if you are covered.

Some estimates state that as many as 30% to 40% of drivers do not have insurance. If you are involved in an accident with one of these drivers and sue them for damages, you may win and obtain a judgment. The problem is that the other driver may not have any assets, thereby making the judgment practically worthless. If you have uninsured motorist insurance you wouldn't have to be concerned because your insurance protects you. The maximum amount of uninsured motorist insurance that you can obtain is $100,000.00, and if you can afford the premium it is a wise investment.

You should always have an attorney advise you of your rights pertaining to uninsured motorist insurance. Insurance companies often use clauses trying to limit their liability which can be overturned or negotiated by your attorney. For example, if you have multiple cars, your coverage would be expanded to $100,000.00 per car, and motorcycles that are not listed on the policy could also be covered. In addition, children or other family members may also be covered on your policy under certain circumstances.

WRONGFUL DEATH

Q. *What are the requisites and damages recoverable in a wrongful death action?*

A. (A) *FILING SUIT.*

    1. The only party who is qualified to bring a wrongful death action in

the State of Florida is the personal representative of the estate. The personal representative must meet certain requirements as established by Florida law.

(B) *STATUTE OF LIMITATIONS:*

1. The action for a wrongful death must be brought within two years from the date of death to comply with the Statute of Limitations. However, it may be suspended in some cases regarding the death of the personal representative.

(C) *VENUE:*

1. Venue usually lies in the county in which the decedent was domiciled before his death, or the county in which the decedent was possessed of property or had creditors. Occasional proper venue may be established where the negligent act occurred.

(D) *PERSONS ENTITLED TO RECOVER:*

1. Those that may be entitled to recover are qualified "survivors" including decedent's spouse, minor children, parents (if the decedent was a minor) and other wholly dependent blood relatives. Adopted brothers and sisters may also qualify.

(E) *DAMAGES:*

1. Wrongful death damages are determined by a jury. The following are a few of the categories available for damages:

    (a) Loss of support and services;

    (b) Mental pain and suffering;

    (c) Loss of companionship;

    (d) Medical or funeral expenses;

    (e) Punitive damages;

    (f) Loss of employment income.

2. Damages vary from case to case, depending on circumstances, age of the deceased and many other factors.

(F) *EXPERT WITNESSES:*

1. Normally an economist will testify as to the value of the different categories above and how inflationary trends will effect support of the future.

DAMAGES FOR PERSONAL INJURIES

Q. *Could you briefly explain the types of damages that are allowable in personal injury cases?*

A. Each personal injury case is different and thus each case has different types of damages. Some of the damages that *may* be recovered are as follows:

- Any expense that may be necessary to effect a cure may be recovered if the reasonableness and necessity are proven.

- A spouse or parent can recover medical expenses in effecting or attempting to cure injuries for either spouse or minor child.
- Future medical expenses may be awarded if they are imminent or a reasonable probability exists that they will be incurred.
- Payment of medical expenses from an independent or collateral source (insurance) does not lessen the damages that may be recovered.
- Physical pain and suffering awards are usually determined by a jury and all factors are usually considered such as intensity and duration of pain, and type of injury. Many factors can make up the decision as to amount of the award for physical pain and suffering.
- Mental pain and anguish are generally not allowed unless there has been physical impact from an external force. Some of the considerations involved in this aspect of damages include effect of injury on health, diminished capacity for enjoying life, destruction or impairment of physical functions, mental health before injury, etc.
- Damages can be obtained for loss of earnings and profits and the injured party must show proof of losses due to an inability to work.
- Damages of impairment of earning capacity may be also be obtained if medical testimony can be established showing an effect on earning capacity.
- Loss of conjugal fellowship (consortium) can also be grounds for damages in a personal injury case.
- Humiliation and embarrassment are also grounds for damages if there has been a disfigurement or injured party has been embarrassed from an assault and battery.

SOCIAL SECURITY DISABILITY CLAIMS

Q. *Who is eligible to receive disability benefits from Social Security?*

A. First, a definition of the word "disability" in the Social Security Act: The "inability to engage in any substantial gainful activity by reason of any medically determinable physical or mental impairment which can be expected to last for a continuous period of not less than 12 months."

The Act also provides that an individual (except widow, surviving divorced wife, or widower) can be determined to be under disability only if such physical or mental impairments are of such severity that he/she is not only unable to do his/her previous work but cannot engage in any other kind of substantial gainful work which exists in the national economy.

Widows, surviving divorced wives or widowers shall not be determined to be under disability unless his or her physical or mental impairments are of a level of severity which under regulations prescribed by the Social Security Secretary is deemed to be sufficient to preclude an individual from engaging in any gainful activity.

Disabilities shall not be allowed by the Social Security Act unless proper medical evidence to support the claims are presented and proven and the Social Security Administrator may require as much evidence as needed to satisfy the claim.

Disabled widows are treated a little differently in that factors such as age, education and past work experience are evaluated differently in determining their claims.

In deciding the value of claims the Social Security has published a Listing of Impairments and then such impairments must be proven.

The process involved in disability claims, simply stated, is as follows:

1. Filing the claim—pre-hearing stage:
   (a) Filling out disability forms;
   (b) Filling out work history;
   (c) Selecting appropriate state agency;
   (d) Etc.
2. Pre-Hearing preparation:
3. Hearing:
   (a) Reviewing medical history;
   (b) Clarifying type of disability;
   (c) Witnesses;
   (d) Etc.
4. Post hearing activity:
5. Appeals (if necessary):

Social Security Disability claims require the careful preparation of one's case by a competent attorney. Many attorneys specialize in this field.

RIGHT TO DIE OR DEATH WITH DIGNITY

Q. *Do I have the "right to die" once my body could only be kept alive by mechanical means?*

A. Yes. There are presently 39 states that have enacted some form of legislation described as a "Living Will," "natural death," or "right to die" statutes.

The common element in these states is that if a doctor relies upon a written statement, properly executed, which states that a person does not wish his life sustained by artificial or mechanical means after his body reached a medical level of being unable to support itself, then the doctor would be immune from criminal and/or unprofessional conduct for stopping treatment on the individual.

Florida passed similar legislation on May 29, 1984. The common law right of bodily self-determination has long been recognized. Justice Cardoza once said, "Every human being of adult years and sound mind has a right to determine what shall be done with his body."

Some states hold that decisions to terminate life support systems must be submitted to the court for its determination of what is best for the patient.

The most significant effect of a Living Will in states that have not passed right to die legislation, would be that it would serve as a persuasive document directed toward the family and physician by expressing the person's desires as to whether or not he wished to be mechanically supported when there was no hope of survival and the illness was terminal. In some cases doctors may be liable for damages and costs when they expressly disregard a person's wishes and continue extraordinary medical treatment against one's wishes.

A Living Will can be useful for family members who may be in a dilemma as to what course of action they should take at a moment of crisis or decision making. Written instructions as to death wishes ease the burden of family members and doctors.

A Living Will must have two or more witnesses and it should be notarized. If properly executed it may be valid even if a person is declared incompetent, if the person was competent at its signing. Witnesses should be unrelated to the declarant and not a potential heir to the estate.

In states that recognize Living Wills, oral revocations as well as written revocations are recognized.

SUMMARY: Living Wills are formally recognized in Florida. If one was in existence and a decision has to be made regarding extraordinary medical support or life-sustaining measures, such a document would be used by family and medical personnel to help in the decision-making process.

A Living Will should be considered as a supplement to your present Will or Trust.

ANATOMICAL GIFTS

Q. *What procedure must I follow if I wish to give all or part of my body at death?*

A. A gift of all or part of one's body, to be effective at death, may be made by Will. An important consideration in this method is that the donation need not wait for probate of the document to become effective. Such a delay, of course, would make the gift useless, as probate takes a considerable amount of time.

Possible problems that could influence the court on the disposition of a part of the body are:

1. Statutory authorization of the intended disposition;
2. Reasonableness of the requested disposition;
3. Degree of clarity and exactness in making the request.

Factors which tend to influence a court to strike an intended testamentary directive include:

1. Contrary wishes of the decedent's spouse and/or family.
2. Impossibility or impracticability of complying due to destruction of the body;
3. Conflicting statements of decedent as to intent of actual disposition;
4. Competency at the time of the disposition.

BEST WAY: Perhaps the best way to make a gift of all or part of one's body may be made by the execution of a card or specific document to that effect. No formal words are required, but the card indicating the desire to make a gift must be witnessed by at least two witnesses and preferably a notary public.

This manner of donation offers the advantage of speedy execution and the gifts also tend to remain somewhat more private. The gift card should be carried in a wallet or purse and failure to do so could imply a revocation of the gifts.

Some states provide for the execution of an anatomical gift by completion of a statement on the reverse of the operators and chauffeurs license.

OTHER FACTORS: *Generally speaking, oral promises of an anatomical donation are not enforceable.

*Persons must be of sound mind and be at least 18 years of age when making a donation.

*Certain statutory provisions now have created a hierarchy of power of persons empowered to make donations of portions of a decedent's body. The list begins with the decedent's spouse, passing through certain relatives and ending with any person under right or obligation to see to the disposition of the body.

Finally, your decision to make an anatomical gift should be made "public" to your family, friends and attorney in order to avoid confusion upon your death. You should consult your local attorney for the best way to achieve your objectives.

TORTS

Q. *Please define what a "Tort" is.*

A. I will never forget, while in law school and registering for the first semester of classes, how many first-year students did not know what a "Tort" was.

A really satisfactory definition of a tort has yet to be found. The broad definitions of the word also encompass other matters in addition to torts and the narrow definitions generally are not sufficient.

The word "Tort" comes from the Latin word, "tortus" which means twisted, crooked—not straight. Some general, common definitions of tort are:

    (a) Act or omission, not a mere breach of contract, causing injury to another . . .

    (b) Torts arise from breach of *duty* primarily fixed by the laws;

    (c) A civil wrong for which the remedy is a common law action for unliquidated damages;

    (d) An act or omission which unlawfully violates a person's right created by law.

A tort is not the same thing as a crime as criminals are prosecuted to protect the public at large, whereas torts are a civil action commenced by the injured party, himself or herself.

Perhaps the best way to define "Torts" is to break some of them into categories and give examples.

    1. Intentional interference with person and property: Included in this category are battery, assault, trespass, infliction of mental distress and false imprisonment and conversion.
    2. Defamation: Libel, slander and other forms of defamation.
    3. Invasion of privacy.
    4. Nuisance (public and private).
    5. Products Liability: negligence, warranty, unsafe products.
    6. Economic Relations: Interference with contractual relations, interference with prospective advantage.
    7. Misuse of Legal Procedure: Malicious prosecution, wrongful civil proceedings, abuse of process.

There are many other forms of "Torts" and any questions should be directed to your attorney.

DOG BITES

Q. *What remedies do I have against the owner of a dog that bit me?*

A. The answer to this question can only be given in general terms. The first assumption I will make is that the dog was tame and not wild. Owners of any type of animals (dogs, snakes, chimpanzees, etc.) are absolutely liable for injuries caused.

Owners of tame dogs are liable for compensatory damages and may be liable for damages for shock and fright, pain and suffering even though the damages might only include a slight scar.

In cases where there is substantial injury, such as a permanent injury or serious deforming scars, persons may be entitled to large recovery. Many factors are used in determining award in cases such as this, including but not limited to loss of earnings, medical expenses, deformities, pain and suffering and shock and fright.

Generally, the dog's owner is responsible for the damage caused, and it is a "myth" that a dog has one free bite. The element of the owner's knowledge of the dog's "dangerous nature" is not forgiven even if the dog had never previously bitten anyone. However, dog owners are not usually liable when the person bitten has mischievously or carelessly provoked or aggravated the dog and the dog then caused the damage.

Owners may avoid some of the liability by placing a sign on their property such as "BEWARE OF DOG", "BAD DOG" or "DANGEROUS DOG". A customary defense of the owner is assumption of the risk, stating that the bitten person assumed the risks.

There are many cases where injuries are caused by a dog chasing a child into the street and the child is then struck by an oncoming vehicle, or cars swerving to miss hitting a dog and thereby causing an accident. These cases are decided individually and solely upon the facts of each case.

There are also many interesting cases about infectious dogs causing damage. It is a felony for a veterinarian or an owner of domestic animals afflicted or suffering with a contagious, infectious or communicable disease not to report such disease to the Department of Agriculture and Consumer Service.

SLIP & FALL

Q. *Is a business owner automatically responsible if you fall while on his property?*

A. No. Many lawsuits arise out of defective conditions of premises or negligence in maintaining premises which allegedly result in injury to patrons. These are called slip and fall or trip cases. The business owner is not automatically liable in slip and fall cases.

Liability may fall upon an owner when an area is improperly lighted, improperly built or designed, or upon which some obstruction or foreign matter has been placed. Liability may also occur due to failure to warn patrons of dangerous conditions, failure to repair, or negligence in repairs. In most cases, it will be necessary to prove some negligence, omission, or failure to act on the part of the business owner before the business owner can be found liable.

If the patron fell on his own due to some medical problem or due to his own clumsiness, the business owner would not be responsible. Let's examine a hypothetical case where X came out of an apartment building and tripped down the stairway at 8:30 p.m., resulting in severe injuries to her head, body and limbs. She sues the apartment complex and would probably allege:

1. The owner failed to properly light the stairway;
2. The lights that were there were not turned on at the time of the accident;
3. The stairway was unsafe and dangerous and was constructed in a manner which caused the accident;

X sues for damages for pain and suffering, past and future, for permanent disabilities, and for doctor and hospital bills.

The owner counters and states that X was contributorily negligent in that she was not looking where she was going, and that (poor) lighting of the stairway was not the direct cause of the accident. The history of the owner as to other slip and fall occurrences could be important as to the frequency of such accidents.

In such a case the judge or jury will obviously decide the outcome, and if X prevails, they will also decide to what extent. If X were to prevail, factors such as the extent of the personal injury, days absent from work, and medical expenses would all be important.

Cases against grocery store chains pertaining to a customer's slipping on a wet spot where a spill occurred are very common and are decided on a case-by-case basis. Each slip and fall or personal injury case is decided based on its own set of circumstances and factors. If you have been injured due to a slip and fall, you should see your attorney.

SWIMMING POOL ACCIDENTS

Q. *If I am injured in a swimming pool, what rights do I have against the owner?*

A. Your rights depend upon many factors, but let's begin with whether it is a public or private swimming pool.

The liability of an owner/operator of a public swimming pool is founded on common law concepts of negligence. The operator does not guarantee the patron's safety but has the legal status of an operator of an amusement or recreational activity who extends an open invitation to the public. There is a duty to exercise ordinary care for the protection of patrons and to provide the premises and equipment safe for the purposes for which it was designed or could reasonably be expected to be used. The operator usually has a duty to inspect for damages, to discover and eliminate defects or dangers, and to supervise activities in and around the pool in order to safeguard patrons from natural hazards, including the actions and conduct of other patrons.

Owners of private (home) pools have a slightly different duty to their guests and usually have the duty to refrain from active negligence and to warn of a known danger. The guest, for the most part, assumes the ordinary risks that attach to the premises.

The most common accidents range from comparatively minor bruises and abrasions to serious disabilities such as a broken neck and severed spinal cord, injury to the brain, or even death from drowning. The liability of a landowner for accidents resulting in injuries to trespassing children under the attractive nuisance doctrine has been expanded through the years. Each case must be analyzed on its own merits as to liability in matters such as these.

Comparative negligence is often used as a defense in these types of cases whereby the defendant states that the actions of the plaintiff directly resulted in the accident and that the defendant should not be held liable for the negligent actions of the plaintiff.

In public swimming pools the most common allegations are negligence in the failure to provide safe facilities, failure to provide sufficient lifeguards, and failure to alleviate overcrowding of the pool.

If you have been injured in a swimming pool, you should see an attorney to determine your rights.

PRODUCT LIABILITY

Q. *Are product liability lawsuits hard to prove?*

A. Some attorneys will tell you that all lawsuits are hard to prove. Product liability cases often involve technical evidence in specialized fields such as engineering, physics and electronics. Much of the evidence is hard for jurors to understand, and they must be educated on the subject as well as the merits of the case.

Many product liability cases are based on the defendant's inadequate directions or failure to warn of the dangers of the product. Cases are also based on the assumption that once a product is manufactured, it will work properly and that it is not harmful.

120

Let's examine a case where plaintiff was injured when an automobile jack failed in its use. The jack was manufactured by the U.S. Jack Company, sold to General Auto Manufacturer, and then sold as an accessory to Local Car Dealer. Plaintiff then bought the car from dealer with a new car warranty. Plaintiff was injured while under the car and the jack stripped or collapsed and the automobile fell upon plaintiff, pinning him under the vehicle and injuring him.

In the above case plaintiff would have to show the court that the jack failed to perform and was in a defective condition at the time it left the manufacturer and at the time it left the local dealer. Plaintiff should also show that the defective condition rendered the jack unreasonably dangerous and that all of the defendant's should be held strictly liable for plaintiff's injuries as a result of the unreasonable defective condition. Plaintiff will also try to prove that the design and the manufacturing process were defective, and that the jack was not inspected before delivery.

Plaintiff will seek damages for extensive injuries, including past and future pain and suffering, medical bills, past lost earnings, loss of future earnings, and costs of court.

Each product liability case is different, but each case must prove that the plaintiff was injured due to the defendant's negligence, i.e. defective product, manufacture or design, and that such negligence was the proximate cause of the plaintiff's injuries thereby entitling plaintiff to recover his damages from defendant as a result of this negligence.

BUSINESS AND REAL ESTATE

EMPLOYEE OR INDEPENDENT CONTRACTOR

Q. *What are the advantages and disadvantages of being an independent contractor versus an employee?*

A. The best way to answer this question is to analyze the differences between an employee and an independent contractor.

1. Employers have the general right to dismiss employees for cause whereas independent contractors are controlled by contractual agreement whether it be written or implied.
2. Payment to employees is generally made periodically or by the hour. Payment to independent contractors is made by the quote or by the job.
3. An employee is assumed to have a more permanent relationship than an independent contractor who is assumed to have a limited relationship.
4. Employees usually have all tools and equipment paid for and all overhead paid. Employees may not hire other employees to assist them unless previously agreed to. Independent contractors supply their own equipment and tools unless otherwise agreed upon and are given opportunity for profit or loss. They have the right to employ others to assist them.

    Court cases have determined independent contractors supply their own employees where employers have controlled the way work was performed, provided all tools and paid all overhead expenses.
5. Employers may restrict outside employment of employees, but no such restrictions can be placed on independent contractors because their services are offered to the general public.

Substantial liabilities for FICA taxes and withholding can build up unless employers have a reasonable basis for treating an individual as an independent contractor.

Business owners should investigate turning over certain operations to independent contractors who may be able to perform services at an overall lower net cost.

Independent contractors always have the following characteristics:

- No salary;
- No payroll taxes;
- Less supervision;
- Easier termination (by agreement).

Employees are subject to:

- Federal income tax withholding;
- FICA taxes withheld and employer contribution to Social Security;
- State and Federal unemployment taxes.

Caution should always be taken by one who has a relationship with an independent contractor. For example, real estate brokers who control the hours of independent contractors (salesmen) and pay their overhead expenses, have been found to have employees (not independent contractors) and therefore subject to the above taxes. You should consult your attorney to discuss this matter if you have any concerns.

SELLER'S SECURITY

Q. *If I sell my business, how can I assure myself that I will receive all my money from the sale?*

A. I would assume from your question that the buyer has asked you to hold a mortgage or promissory note. A *few* of the precautions you can take are as follows:

MORTGAGE: If real property is involved, be sure to get a mortgage instead of a promissory note. This will make you a "secured creditor" which will be extremely important if the business ever went bankrupt.

CHATTEL MORTGAGE: Secure a "chattel mortgage" and list the assets of the sale on the schedule that attaches to the mortgage. This will give you additional security and give you a better position if the business faces difficulties and is unable to pay you.

ASSIGNMENT OF PROFITS: Assignment of profits will give you certain rights to receive profits if you ever have to "foreclose" the above mentioned mortgages. Thus, if the buyer is in default or violation of his other agreements, you will automatically have the rights to income and profits because of his default.

UCC: As additional security, you will want to file a UCC-1 form with the Secretary of State. This form will list all of the secured items of the sale and make them a matter of public record. Since both parties sign the form, the question of whether the items are secured cannot be challenged.

LEASE: If the business is operating from a leased facility, be sure to get the landlord to execute an assignment of lease or a release of lease, with the buyer obtaining a new lease.

AS IS: For additional protection, the buyer should sign a statement of understanding that the business is "as is" and no further warranties are given particularly to inventory and equipment.

ADDITIONAL POINTS: You should also get the buyer to acknowledge his responsibility to undertake the following acts and agree to hold seller harmless from any and all liability arising from any failure to undertake or complete same:

(a) Advertising under fictitious name;

(b) Obtaining IRS identification number;

(c) Obtaining insurance coverage, if desired;

(d) Transferring license and permits;

(e) Obtaining sales tax permit.

CASH: Of course, the very best deal you could make would be to receive cash for your business and then security would not be a problem.

TITLE INSURANCE

Q. *Why is title insurance necessary and why do so many banks or lenders require it?*

A. Title insurance is very much misunderstood and probably one of the most complained about types of insurance. There are many reasons a title should be researched for protection of the parties in a real estate transaction.

Owners title insurance generally pays for the defense of your title against the following (partial list) types of claims and will protect you against hidden risks:

- Types of forgery;
- Types of fraud concerning the execution of documents;
- Undue influence on a grantor or executor;
- False personation by those purporting to be owners of the property;
- Marital status incorrectly represented;
- Missing or undisclosed heirs;
- Last Will & Testament improperly probated;
- Fraudulent or mistaken interpretation of Wills and Trusts;
- Conveyance of mental incompetent;
- Conveyance by a minor;
- Subsequent heirs to an estate;
- Improper or inadequate surveys;
- Improper, incorrect or misleading legal descriptions;
- Non-delivery of deeds;
- Claims of unsatisfied claims or invoices not shown on the public records;
- Deeds executed under expired or fraudulent powers of attorney;

- Claims due to mistaken or similar names;
- Claims due because of dower or courtesy rights of ex-spouses;
- Deliverance of deeds after the death of a grantor;
- Clerical errors and improper or incorrect indexing.

Of course, title insurance gives you knowledge of unsatisfied mortgages, liens, judgments or other *recorded* claims against the property. Title policies also advise about easements, restrictions and other existing covenants.

Banks and lenders require title insurance because they want to be equally protected and make sure that the money loaned to a buyer is being loaned for a good, sound investment and that the buyer will not have incentives to walk away from the property because of unknown problems at the time of sale.

CONDOMINIUM LAW

Q. *What area should I be cautious about when purchasing a condominium?*

A. One of the most important elements in the decision making of purchasing a condominium is the thorough study of the prospectus. It gives the vital information about the terms of sale, description of the property and legal documents about the property. It will advise you of a potential roof or termite problem and give dates of recent repairs to such items. It will document and list all pertinent information concerning the condominium and the associated risks. The prospectus is required by law to be given to a potential buyer and you will probably sign a document stating that you received one.

Other information contained in the prospectus are estimates of the maintenance costs. The age of the building and the equipment will be important here because buyers that have to replace an elevator or roof could be caught short. Low maintenance fees could be a warning of potential traps for unsuspecting buyers. Other areas to watch for are rules governing living arrangements and pets, information of the background of the developer and other persons involved with the project, and what guarantees are being offered with the sale of the property. It can also settle questions regarding subletting the condominium, i.e. whether or not it is permissible.

In the area of financing for the purchase of a condominium you should always make your condominium purchase contingent upon financing if you are unsure of loan availability. The balance due at closing, amount of downpayment should be closely scrutinized and discussed with your attorney.

Always schedule a walk-through prior to closing as you would in any real estate closing. Do this before you sign the contract closing the transaction.

Another must in the purchase of any property is title insurance. It is relatively inexpensive insurance for the assurance that the title is free of problems.

Minor but important things to consider in condominium purchasing are parking privileges, outdoor cooking privileges, and definitions of your interest in the common areas of the condominium.

Again, your most important document is the prospectus and it is often several hundred pages long. It should be reviewed by your attorney who can analyze potential problems for you.

CONTRACTS

Q. *Please distinguish between the different types of contracts that one may enter into.*

A. Generally, the term "contract" can be defined as a promise or promises for which the law gives a remedy or the performance of which the law gives a duty which is based on sufficient consideration.

EXPRESS OR IMPLIED

Contracts may be express or implied. Contracts are usually *express* when the terms are stated or written by the parties and *implied* when the terms are not so stated. Express contracts and implied contracts are based upon mutual consent.

There is a greater burden upon Plaintiffs who rely upon implied contracts to prove their case as one who was interested in protecting himself had the opportunity to protect himself to a greater degree.

VOID AND VOIDABLE CONTRACTS

Voidable contracts are valid and binding upon the parties until it is avoided by the party entitled to avoid it. This type contract can be affirmed or rejected at the election of one of the parties. It is binding if the parties affirm it, but of no effect if rejected by one party.

Other examples of voidable contracts are those induced by fraud and misrepresentation, duress, contracts made by infants or incompetent persons.

FORMATION OF CONTRACTS

For a valid contract there must be at least two parties, a capacity to contract, mutual assent of the same thing at the same time, meeting of the minds, offer, acceptance, definiteness and certainty, definition of duration of time, and consideration.

QUASI CONTRACTS

Quasi contracts are generally those "implied in law or constructive contracts." Whereas express or implied contracts rely upon the mutual assent of the parties, quasi contracts rely upon the legal remedies available where parties are unjustly enriched or parties have arrived at some benefit where they should be legally charged. For example, the law implies a promise to pay when money is advanced by one for another's use and benefit at the latter's request. Another example is when a sub-contractor has the right of collection against a property owner.

EXECUTORY OR EXECUTED CONTRACTS

An *executory* contract is one in which a party binds himself to perform a task whereas an *executed* contract is one in which the object of the agreement has been performed and everything that was to be done has been done. Contracts may be partly executed or partly executory or may be executory as to one part and executed as to the other.

UNILATERAL AND BILATERAL CONTRACTS

Bilateral contracts are, in general terms, based on mutual promises to do something in the future in which consideration has been established. *Unilateral* contracts are not based on mutual promises. For example, a letter to an attorney requesting services is a unilateral contract when the attorney performs the services and thus a fee is due.

Note: Proper information on the explanation of contracts could take a textbook. Consult your local attorney for any questions you have in the area of contracts.

CORPORATIONS

Q. *What are the procedures, advantages and costs of incorporating myself or my business?*

A. Basic corporations are established by filing Articles of Incorporation with the Secretary of State. The information needed for the Articles of Incorporation and a short explanation are as follows:

1. *NAME OF THE CORPORATION:*
   Your corporation may not have the same name as another existing corporation in Florida. Generally speaking, your attorney will do a name check before filing the Articles of Incorporation.
2. *CORPORATION'S EXISTENCE:*
   A corporation is a separate entity and the Articles generally state the existence shall continue thereafter in perpetuity.
3. *GENERAL PURPOSE:*
   General purposes of corporations are usually for any or all lawful business permitted any corporation under the Florida General Corporation Act, but can be for one specific purpose.

4. *STOCK:*

The corporation must have a specific number of common stock and each shall have a specified par value.

5. *PREEMPTIVE RIGHTS:*

Shareholders may be entitled in the Articles to have preemeptive rights with respect to any unissued or treasury shares of ownership.

6. *REGISTERED AGENT:*

The corporation must have a registered agent or someone who will receive summonses (service from sheriff) if the corporation is sued. Change of agent or address must always be reported to the Secretary of State.

7. *BOARD OF DIRECTORS:*

The corporation must list the initial board of directors and their addresses.

8. *INCORPORATOR:*

The name and address of the incorporator must be listed in the Articles.

SOME ADVANTAGES OF A CORPORATION:

The main advantage of a corporation is limited liability of shareholders that protect personal belongings. Other advantages include the tax benefits of "writing off" hospital bills, doctor bills, dental bills, medical and hospital insurance, disability insurance and other types of benefits. There are other tax write-offs available that are not usually written off by individuals.

SOME DISADVANTAGES OF A CORPORATION

The main disadvantages of a corporation are the certain types of taxes it must pay. For example, corporations pay higher social security taxes than a sole proprietor and must pay unemployment taxes not chargeable to a sole proprietor. However, the overall tax structure of a corporation can be lower if properly planned.

COST OF INCORPORATING:

The filing fee with the State is $63.00 and a corporate book which includes a corporate seal and the issuance of stock is $38.00 to $50.00. Attorney fees vary depending upon the complexity of the incorporation and the services rendered.

SUGGESTION:

See your attorney about incorporating your hobby for tax savings.

INSTALLMENT SALES

Q. *Could you explain the important provisions of the Installment Sales revision Act of 1980?*

A. The installment sales method of reporting income is to permit the spreading of the income tax over the period during which payments of the sales price are received. By using the installment sales method, it alleviates possible liquidity problems which might arise from the bunching of gain in the year of sale when a portion of the selling price has not been actually received.

Under the Act, the basic rules for sales of real property and casual sales of personal property are contained in the Internal Revenue Code of 1954, as amended (I.R.C. Section 453). Section 453A contains the rules covering dealer transactions in personal property. Section 453B contains the rules covering dispositions of installment obligations. Prior to the Installment Sales Revision Act of 1980, all of the rules concerning installment sales were contained in Section 453.

The new Act eliminates a provision of the prior law which stated that no more than 30 percent of the selling price be received in the taxable year of the sale to qualify for installment sales reporting. Under the new law, amount of payment in the year of the sale is irrelevant. All sales of realty and nondealer personal property will automatically be considered installment sales, no matter how much is received in the year of the sale, unless the taxpayer elects otherwise.

The Act eliminates the requirement that a deferred payment sale be for two or more payments. Under the new law, only one payment will be necessary, so long as it is made in a taxable year after the year of the sale. This will allow a sale to be eligible for installment treatment even if the entire purchase price is to be paid in a single lump sum in a year subsequent to the taxable year of the sale. (Example: Calendar Year taxpayer—sale made during 1981—no payments in year of sale—payment in full 1982—in such a sale, gain will be taxed entirely in 1982, even though sale took place in 1981).

The Act eliminates the requirement that the selling price for casual sales of personal property must exceed $1,000 to qualify for installment sale reporting. No minimum sales price is mentioned under the new law.

The Act further provides that the installment sale method of reporting is automatic unless the taxpayer elects not to have the installment sale treatment apply. This is exactly the opposite of the prior law which resulted in considerable litigation over what constituted a valid and timely installment sale election.

The installment sales provisions relate to installment reporting of gains and do not affect the time for recognizing losses from the sale or exchange of property for deferred payments. Losses cannot be reported on the installment plan.

PARTNERSHIPS

Q. *Should I form a partnership with a friend?*

A. The advantages of a partnership are that one of the parties can donate either time, money, or expertise that the other parties do not have. However, even all three of those elements may not be sufficient for the success of a partnership.

Partnerships have a higher failure rate than sole proprietors or corporations, and many partnerships fail within the first year or two. Therefore, it is very important to have a written partnership agreement which spells out exactly what will happen when one of the partners dies or decides to terminate the agreement. There should be a detailed checklist of what happens to capital equipment, cash on hand, and goodwill when the partnership terminates.

A good planning tool for a partnership is a buy-sell agreement. This is an agreement which can be funded through life insurance and protects one's investment upon death and insures family members or other business partners of enough monies to continue the business or support a family. Partnerships require special tax record-keeping which sometimes is an extra burden that the sole proprietor does not have. Attorneys who draw partnership agreements have checklists of the provisions which should be spelled out to avoid common pitfalls.

Special estate planning techniques should also be considered when a partner draws a Will or a Trust to clearly identify what happens to partnership assets. In some cases it may be advisable to "freeze" partnership interests between family members to save on estate taxes. As you can see, there are many aspects in partnership planning for which the average person will need competent counsel to assist them.

ADVERSE POSSESSION

Q. *Can a neighbor claim any of my property under an "adverse possession" law?*

A. Adverse possession is defined as the open and notorious possession and occupation of real property under an evident claim or color of right. For example, if your neighbor has built a structure on your property and can meet the prerequisite requirements, he may claim your property by filing an adverse possession law suit. The requirements for the acquisition of title by adverse possession are notoriety of possession, hostility, continuity and exclusiveness. Each of the above will be discussed below.

The period of time within which to make an adverse possession claim is seven years with certain exceptions. One of the exceptions is a 20-year period from the recording of a deed or the probate of a Will to convey real property, no person shall assert any claim to the property against claimants under the deed or Will or their successors in title. In Florida, the common-law period of 20 years holds as to the acquisition of a prescriptive right. In order to establish an easement by prescription, a claimant must prove actual, continuous and uninterrupted use for a period of 20 years.

HOSTILITY: In order to establish possession you must show that the property was held adversely and hostilely for the statutory period. Hostile in this sense is defined as possession an exclusive right to the property. For example, possession is not hostile or adverse if permission is given by the owner.

CONTINUOUS POSSESSION & EXCLUSIVENESS: The possession of the property must be continuous and uninterrupted. In general, once adverse possession has begun it may only be interrupted by an ouster, actual or constructive. The doctrine of tacking has been adopted in Florida and successive possessions of several persons may be allowed if the requisite privity exists.

WHO CAN ACQUIRE TITLE? In general, all persons, artificial as well as natural, for example, corporations and municipalities, may acquire property. It has been held that family members *may not* acquire adverse possession against each other without a stronger burden of proof of a hostile holding. Also, husband and wife cannot generally acquire land by adverse possession against the other. The possession of a Trustee is not generally adverse to making a claim under adverse possession.

If you have an adverse possession question, you should see your attorney. The subject is much too complicated to have a complete understanding from this writing.

OVERHANGING LIMBS

Q. *My neighbor's tree has limbs that are overhanging on my property. What can I do?*

A. Property owners may put their land to any reasonable and lawful use that they desire as long as it does not deprive the adjoining landowner of any right or enjoyment of his property. Generally landowners may have trees or shrubbery on their land, and the adjoining landowners do not have a complaint at law to prohibit such trees or shrubbery. Typically, adjoining landowners do not have a cause of action for deprivation of light, air, or view.

It is commonly held that where a tree is located so near the line that the branches overhang and the roots encroach upon the adjoining property, such branches and roots constitute a nuisance which the adjoining landowner may remove. However, the removal of the tree branches should not be such as to destroy the entire tree.

Regarding leaves and other debris, each landowner is responsible for his lawn's maintenance, care and upkeep. If a neighbor causes a severe problem, a possible solution would be to file a public or private nuisance lawsuit. Action of this type should only be taken as a last resort.

There is no invasion of rights of others when one uses his own land lawfully and such use is deemed to be reasonable. Each case, however, should be evaluated as to legal and equitable principles.

Generally, the law does not interfere with a landowner who may put his property to any reasonable and lawful use, as long as his activity is not deemed to be a nuisance. In most cases, the law does not become involved with property owners who lawfully and reasonably use their land even if it would diminish the value of an adjoining lot. Of course, here again, each case would have to be evaluated on its own set of circumstances. Another possible remedy against adjoining landowners is "trespass." Some common examples of this would be to allow fire or water to negligently spread to another's land.

For a full explanation of your rights you should consult your attorney.

FORECLOSURE

Q. *Having been unemployed for nine months and unable to make my house payments resulted in my being served a summons in a foreclosure action. Can you please summarize the events that will happen over the next few months?*

A. Foreclosures have been occurring at a record pace the last few years due to the previously high interest rates and high unemployment figures. The most critical thing for you to do is to have an attorney file an answer to the foreclosure. You have 20 days from the receipt of the summons to file an answer or a default will be entered against you. If a default is entered, the foreclosing petitioner will take the next steps to have the property sold. If you are the only party to the lawsuit, the property *could* be sold on the courthouse steps within 60 days from the time of default.

If times have been bad and you have other judgments against you which have been certified by the clerk, then the petitioner will also have to name those creditors as parties to the lawsuit and foreclose their interests which would have automatically attached to the property being foreclosed.

A "Notice of Sale" has to appear in a local newspaper on two consecutive weeks before the property can be sold. The mortgagor can buy the property if it chooses, and take a deficiency judgment against you for the difference between the total amount due including legal costs, costs of the sale plus back taxes and other costs associated with the foreclosure proceeding and the selling price.

One thing that your attorney can try in your behalf is to "stipulate" to the fact that you are delinquent in your payments and that you promise to bring the mortgage current within a period of time (for instance, 90 days). If you fail in your efforts to bring the mortgage current, then the petitioner would have a right of foreclosure of the mortgage without further notice to you. Often this is the

133

most logical way to proceed if there is a high expectancy of paying the arrearages.

During the foreclosure process you have certain redemption rights which can be exercised. There are many ramifications to foreclosure matters and any specific questions should be directed to an attorney.

EVICTION

Q. *What are the rules regarding eviction of tenants by landlords?*

A. Landlords may recover possession of dwelling units in three basic methods:

1. The tenant can voluntarily surrender it;
2. The tenant can abandon it:
3. The landlord may get a court order.

For a tenant to surrender or abandon a dwelling unit, the tenant must inform the landlord that he is leaving and preferably leave him the keys to the unit. It can be reasonably presumed by the landlord that the tenant has left if the tenant has abandoned the dwelling for one-half of the term of the lease unless the rent is current or some notice of the absence is given to the landlord.

Generally, the landlord would be safe in assuming that the tenant had abandoned the property if all of the possessions and furniture of the tenant had been removed. If the tenant has not surrendered or abandoned the property, the landlord may not generally change locks, turn off utilities, etc. as these remedies are strictly forbidden and such actions could be cause for criminal penalties or money damages.

For a landlord to effectively evict someone by using court action, he must give notice to the tenant which, depending on the circumstances, would either be a three-day notice or a seven-day notice. After proper notice has been given, the landlord may file an eviction suit. Suit is usually filed in the County Court of where the tenant resides and where the property is situated and the Complaint must be served on the tenant by either the sheriff or some other duly authorized process server.

Since the action is filed in County Court, it is advisable for one to be represented by an attorney. An owner can represent himself in court, but no other agent can represent an owner except an attorney. Only attorneys can represent corporations.

Tenants have five days to answer the Complaint that is served by the sheriff or process server. This excludes Saturdays, Sundays or legal holidays. If the tenant does not leave after receiving the Complaint, the landlord may ask the court for a default and a default judgment. If the tenant files an answer, a hearing must be set before a judge. At the hearing both sides may give appropriate evidence; but if the tenant has a weak case and offers no evidence, the landlord or his attorney may ask for a summary proceeding and get an early judgment. If the tenant does not show up at the hearing, the landlord is entitled to a default and default judgment.

After the landlord or owner has obtained a judgment and the tenant still does not move out, the last remaining process is to obtain the services of a sheriff. This procedure entails going to the clerk of the court, filing a writ of possessions, and taking an extra copy of same to the sheriff. At this point the tenant may be physically removed from the property. The sheriff will not physically help in the removal of the tenant, but he will be on the scene to assist and to protect the landlord during the removal process.

At this point in the procedure the tenant will probably still owe the landlord money for back rent or damages to the property. The final judgment obtained will be effective for 20 years and if the final judgment is certified, it may attach to real property owned by the defendant during the next 20 years. Hopefully, the now-removed tenant will have money one day that will pay off the judgment. Attorney fees generally are not awarded in cases such as this unless a provision in the lease calls for the tenant to pay attorney fees if eviction becomes necessary.

THREE-DAY NOTICE

Q. *What is a three-day notice and how can a landlord evict a tenant who is late with a payment?*

A. If a tenant fails to pay rent when rent is due and the default continues for three days, excluding Saturday, Sunday, and legal holidays, the tenant may be evicted in the following manner:

The landlord will make a written demand for payment of the rent or possession of the premises. If the tenant fails to pay the rent or surrender the premises, the landlord is entitled to a quick hearing under what is known as summary procedure. The three-day notice should take substantially this format:

"You are hereby notified that you are indebted to me in the sum of X dollars for the rent and use of the premises located at XYZ Street, in Pinellas County, Florida, and I demand payment of the rent or possession of the premises within three (3) days (excluding Saturday, Sunday and legal holidays) from the date of delivery of this notice, to wit: on or before the _____ day of _____ 1985, to landlord at the following address: (address)"

The notice may be mailed, or if the tenant is absent from his last or usual place of residence, a copy may be left at the residence. Certified mail is better proof of delivery but is not essential to give effective notice.

Once the proper notice has been served on the tenant, the landlord files a complaint and states the facts concerning the money owed. If the tenant does not contest the facts, the landlord will be entitled to a judgment and the clerk of the court shall issue a writ to the sheriff describing the premises and commanding him to put the landlord in possession after 24 hours notice conspicuously posted on the premises. The prevailing party is entitled to have judgment for costs reimbursed.

If the tenant has abandoned the dwelling unit and has not paid his rent, he will have been deemed to have vacated the premises if he has been absent one-half of the time of the rent cycle. Also, if the tenant holds over and continues in possession after the expiration of the rental agreement without permission of the landlord, the landlord may recover double the amount of the rent due.

A rental agreement without a defined period of time for tenancy may be terminated by either party as follows:

1. If the rent is paid yearly—60 days notice.
2. If the rent is paid quarterly—30 days notice.
3. If the rent is paid monthly—15 days notice.
4. If the rent is paid weekly—7 days notice.

SEVEN-DAY NOTICE

Q. *Can a landlord be given a seven-day notice of termination of a lease?*

A. Yes. A tenant may terminate a rental agreement by giving the landlord a seven-day notice of intention to terminate because of the landlord's failure to comply with material provisions of the lease as stated in the Florida statutes.

The landlord's obligations, unless otherwise agreed upon with the tenant, are to comply with all applicable building, housing and health codes, and if there are no applicable health codes, to maintain the roofs, windows, screens, doors, floors, steps, porches, exterior walls, foundations, and all other structural components. Unless otherwise agreed, the landlord shall be responsible for extermination of rats, mice, roaches, ants, wood-destroying pests, and bedbugs. They are also responsible for heat, running water, and hot water along with locks and keys, and garbage removal.

The landlord is generally given reasonable access to the dwelling unit, and the tenant shall not unreasonably without consent to the landlord to inspect the premises, make repairs, alterations or improvements.

A sample seven-day notice would be similar to the following:

Demand is hereby made that you remedy the noncompliance of the lease signed between X and Y on 1/1/85. After repeated requests you have failed to provide heating (or whatever noncompliance) in Unit 00. Failure on your part to remedy this noncompliance will result in termination of this lease and I will vacate the premises.

The outcome of the above would be as follows:

1. If the landlord's failure to comply renders the unit uninhabitable and the tenant vacates, the tenant shall not be liable for rent during that period.
2. If the landlord's failure to comply does not render the unit uninhabitable and the tenant remains in occupancy, the rent for the period of noncompliance shall be reduced in amount in proportion to the loss of rental value caused by noncompliance.

The landlord can also give a tenant a seven-day notice to vacate the premises for noncompliance. The tenant may usually cure the noncompliance. Items of noncompliance can include simple things such as having unauthorized pets, guests, vehicles, failing to keep premises clean and sanitary or even parking in unauthorized areas.

COURTS & TRIAL

PRE-TRIAL INTERVENTION

Q. *What are the eligibility requirements for the pre-trial intervention program for criminal misdemeanors?*

A. The pre-trial intervention program in Pinellas County is a method that allows accused individuals to by-pass their trial and to keep their case out of the court system. Successful completion of the pre-trial program will result in criminal charges being dismissed and the avoidance of any criminal record of the accused.

The requirements for being accepted for the program are as follows:

1. The person must be charged with a misdemeanor offense only, excluding traffic offenses.
2. First time offenders and those whose criminal record consists of no more than one prior conviction for a non-violent misdemeanor offense.
3. If the case involves a victim, the victim must consent to the defendant entering the program.
4. The approval by the County Court Judge must be obtained.
5. Approval by the Program Administrator must be obtained.
6. Approval by the State Attorney for the Sixth Judicial Circuit of Florida.

The program lasts for a total of six months. During the first three months the defendant is under the active supervision of the Salvation Army Correctional Services Office, and the final three months the defendant is under inactive supervision. The Salvation Army Correctional Services Office is allowed to make a background investigation of the accused. The accused must waive his right to a speedy trial during the duration of the program. If the accused does not successfully complete the program as outlined by the Salvation Army, the State Attorney's Office can end the defendant's participation in the program and the case will be returned for formal prosecution.

The purpose of this program is to meet the needs of the accused for treatment and rehabilitation and to prevent any further involvement by the accused in the criminal justice system. The program also reduces the workload in the court system and allows the system to work more effectively and efficiently. Often the Salvation Army will participate in helping the accused to find worthwhile employment, locating appropriate educational or vocational programs, and providing counseling for any adjustment problems the accused may have. It is a very flexible program that can be structured to meet the needs of the accused and may definitely help him to rehabilitate himself.

This program provides an excellent alternative probation plan with intensive rehabilitative supervision. It is a positive way of having criminal charges dismissed and gives the accused an excellent chance of not having a criminal record.

SMALL CLAIMS COURT

Many businessmen and professionals of all disciplines are unaware of the advantage of "Small Claims Court."

The primary advantage is the settlement of disputes and collection of debts of differences up to $2,500.00. Businessmen and professionals are allowed to represent themselves, if they desire, without the services of an attorney.

The following filing fees are as follows:

For claims up to $99.00..............................Fee $20.00
For claims $100 to $999 ....Fee $30.00
For claims $1,000 to $2,500 ....Fee $35.00

Service of summons by certified mail is $3.00 for each defendant or service by Sheriff is $12.00 for each defendant. If the defendant is outside the State of Florida, you must determine the county and state, the defendant's address, the Sheriff's fee to serve a summons, the Sheriff's address, and if the Sheriff of that county will accept your personal check or if he requires a cashier's check or money order.

The Clerk's Office provides forms to fill out that are self-explanatory that have to be filed with the Court.

You may have a jury trial if you so desire at a cost of $150.00 which amounts to the sum to be paid to the jury. If no demand is made for a jury trial it will be assumed that a jury trial is not desired.

If you are served a summons in a small claims suit, it is possible to file a counter-suit. The claim has to be filed not less than five days prior to the final appearance date. If the counter-claim is in excess of $2,500, the case may be transferred to the next higher court.

At the actual small claims court trial both parties:
(a) Tell their side of the story to the judge;
(b) Ask the other person in the case any questions they wish concerning the claim;
(c) Show papers or photos to explain each side of the story;
(d) Call witnesses to help explain the case.

The final step in the small claims process is the judgment. The part who wins the case is called the judgment creditor and the one who loses the case is called the judgment debtor. The judgment gives the winner additional legal rights such as a lien on the judgment debtor's non-homestead property, the right to have the Sheriff levy on personal property, garnishment rights, and other rights too complex to discuss here.

If you have any questions, you should consult with your attorney or call the Small Claims Division.

CRIMINAL COURT

Q. *I have been charged with a crime and have to go to my "arraignment." Can you explain the steps in the criminal court process?*

A. The first step, of course, is the actual arrest and processing of the accused. Shortly thereafter the accused faces a judge at an "advisory" hearing and the judge will hear the charges, set bond, and advise the accused of his rights.

It is possible that the next step will ROR (Release on Recognizance). This process allows the accused to be released on his own and it is often the case for first-time offenders of less serious crimes.

The arraignment process is the hearing where the defendant or attorney enters the plea. The most common pleas are not guilty, guilty, nolo contendere (no contest). It is unlikely that the defendant will have to be present if represented by an attorney at this stage.

DISCOVERY. The discovery process includes depositions, interrogatories, and other means of producing evidence. Usually during this period both sides offer testimony and evidence to prove their case.

PRE-TRIAL HEARING. This is the meeting of the state's attorney, defense counsel and possibly the defendant to discuss the facts of the case and to, if appropriate, discuss plea-bargaining and possibly a change of plea.

TRIAL. The actual trial may be jury or non-jury at the election is found guilty, the court will order a pre-trial investigation of the defendant's background before the court passes sentence. This background check will show prior records and tends to show the character of the defendant.

PSI—PRE-SENTENCE INVESTIGATION. If the defendant is found guilty, the court will order a pre-trial investigation of the defendant's background before the court passes sentence. This background check will show prior records and tends to show the character of the defendant.

SENTENCING. After considering all the facts of the case including the PSI, the judge will hear final comments of defense counsel and the state's attorney before passing final sentence.

APPEAL. Defense counsel and defendant have 30 days to appeal once sentence is passed.

SPEEDY TRIAL

Q. *What is the law concerning "speedy trials" in Florida?*

A. Speedy trials fall under two categories: upon demand and without demand. Upon demand every person charged with a crime by indictment or information shall have the right to demand a trial within 60 days. The demand is made by filing before the appropriate court a motion for speedy trial and serving it upon the state attorney.

Speedy trials without demand fall under different guidelines. If the crime is a misdemeanor a trial must commence within 90 days. If the crime is a felony the trial must commence within 175 days.

The trial is deemed to have commenced when the trial jury panel is sworn for "voir dire" examination; or if a jury is waived, when the trial proceedings begin before the judge.

If both a felony and misdemeanor are charged against a person and they are consolidated, then the misdemeanor shall be treated as a felony as far as the time rules are concerned for a speedy trial. If the state fails to bring a speedy trial in a misdemeanor case, the defendant may make a motion before the court at the expiration of the prescribed time and be forever discharged from that crime. If the case is a felony, the defendant may also bring a motion for discharge after the expiration of the 175 days. Upon the filing of the motion the court shall hold a hearing on the motion and generally has an additional 10 days to bring the defendant to trial. If the defendant is not brought to trial within the 10 day period, the defendant shall be forever discharged from that crime.

It should be noted that the defendant or defendant's attorney can waive the right for a speedy trial. It is a common practice to waive speedy trials especially if additional time is needed to prepare a defense of the case.

If a prisoner is held outside the state of Florida the speedy trial rules do not generally apply until the person is returned to the jurisdiction in which he is charged and that a proper notice of this fact is filed with the court.

The state attorney cannot drop one charge and charge a defendant with another charge to obtain additional time under speedy trial rules. The crime must be based on the same conduct or criminal episode.

BANKRUPTCY

Q. *Please explain the various types of bankruptcies and the difference between them.*

A. There are three basic types of bankruptcy which will be explained below. Any solvent or insolvent individual, partnership, or corporation may file under Chapter 7 and 11. Only an individual can file under Chapter 13.

1. *Chapter 11 Bankruptcy:*

Basically a Chapter 11 gives a troubled business an opportunity to rehabilitate itself while operating under the protection of the court. A plan or reorganization is created and submitted for vote to the creditors. The plan can call for a controlled liquidation of the estate or the plan can be funded from an infusion of capital from an outside source. If the plan is accepted by the creditors and meets certain statutory requirements, it will be confirmed by the court.

Upon filing a Chapter 11 case, the debtor becomes a debtor-in-possession. Upon showing fraud, gross mismanagement or other grounds, the court may appoint a Trustee. Generally speaking, the debtor-in-possession has the right to deal with its property in the ordinary course of business. Unusual transactions or sales have to be approved by the creditors or court and all parties have to be notified. Once the Chapter 11 is filed with the court, the company has 120 days to submit a plan. A debtor-in-possession may, through its 120-day plan borrow money.

2. *Chapter 13 Bankruptcy:*

Only an individual with regular income may be a debtor under Chapter 13; a corporation or partnership is ineligible. The debtor may have no more than $100,000.00 of unsecured debts and $350,000.00 of secured debts (which includes small businesses owned as sole proprietorships).

A Chapter 13 bankruptcy creates a repayment plan for three years although in some cases they have been known to last for up to five years. A debtor can cure defaults in his home mortgage within a reasonable time under a Chapter 13. Other secured creditors can be renegotiated to the value of their collateral.

3. *Chapter 7 Bankruptcy:*

Only a natural person may receive a discharge under a Chapter 7. Unlike a Chapter 13, the Chapter 7 debtor can only keep $1,000.00 of personal property which becomes exempt. All other property must be sold to help pay debts. Secured parties have superior rights over unsecured claims and are entitled to receive the secured property back or have the property sold for the value owed.

Court Filing Fees:
Chapter 7 or 13—$60.00
Chapter 11—$200.00

Creditors Meeting:
Generally held between 20 to 40 days after attorney files Petition.

BANKRUPTCY DISCHARGE HEARINGS

Q. *What debts are discharged at a bankruptcy hearing?*

A. I assume from your question that you are referring to a Chapter 7 bankruptcy. This type of bankruptcy will discharge most debts except those which are nondischargeable such as certain types of taxes, obligations based on alimony and child support, and certain types of student loans. Most other debts can be totally discharged and released which means that creditors can no longer employ any means to compel or coerce one to repay those debts.

The discharge includes permanent injunctions or prohibition against commencement or continuation of any law suit against a debtor filed by a creditor. Creditors are prohibited to employ informal means of attempting to collect a discharged obligation such as dunning letters, contacting one's employer, or anything else designed to compel or coerce a debtor to repay a discharged obligation.

Employers, government or private, are prohibited to terminate employees because they filed a petition in bankruptcy. Government agencies are also prohibited to refuse to issue drivers licenses or occupational licenses because of filing for bankruptcy.

A discharge has no impact on any liens which represent a valid charge of any property one is retaining after bankruptcy or property one is acquiring after bankruptcy. For example, if a person is buying a house, he may retain his home, if it is a homestead, if he continues to make and keep current the payments. Major appliances may also be retained, but the payments must be kept current if the item is secured. Keep in mind that the debtor (each) can only keep $1,000.00 worth of assets when a bankruptcy is filed.

If you are served with a lawsuit after your bankruptcy hearing, you should notify your attorney immediately. Your creditor should receive a copy of the bankruptcy discharge and an appropriate motion filed before the court.

You cannot be compelled to repay a discharged obligation, but you may voluntarily do so if you desire. You may repay all of it, some of it or none of it. Most bankruptcy clients do not repay debts on a voluntary basis because it would be against their best interests to do so.

Once you receive a bankruptcy discharge you are charged with the responsibility to inform the Trustee if you inherit any money within six months of your discharge. This money would be used to satisfy creditors. You may not file a bankruptcy for a second time within six years from the first filing.

JUDGMENTS

Q. *What is meant by a judgment and what are its ramifications if I have a judgment against me?*

A. Generally speaking, a judgment is a decision of the court based upon the matters submitted to it for adjudication or decision. It is a conclusion of law based on all the facts submitted to the court.

In criminal matters a judgment will mean the defendant is adjudicated guilty or not guilty.

Judgments are also called decrees if they are based on suits in equity.

Although the ramifications of judgments are entirely too large to cover in this article, one of the more important aspects of a judgment is when it becomes a lien against real property. Once a judgment is recorded as a "certified copy" thereof in the county official records, it becomes a judgment on record as a lien against all the real property owned by whoever the judgment is against. As a result of recording the "certified judgment" one can attach to the real property and be entitled to the amount of the judgment at the time of the sale of the property.

The general remedy against a "certified judgment" properly recorded is to take an action in foreclosure. Bankruptcies do not discharge "certified judgments" against properties because they only discharge debts (not judgments) against creditors.

For a judgment to be effective in Florida it must be decreed in a Florida court. Foreign judgments (from other state courts) are usually not effective in Florida and cannot be certified as liens against real property.

Judgment lien attaches only to real property, but it may be transferred to other security. The normal method to find out what another person owns after you receive a judgment is to have your attorney conduct a "deposition in aid of execution." In this deposition, the attorney will find out all the assets of the individual (against whom you have a judgment) and will decide upon which assets to place a lien.

When the property or assets that is subject to the lien of a judgment is converted into cash, the lien attaches to the fund. Thus the judgment holder always has an action against the owner of the property, upon which a lien or certified judgment was placed.

Judgments may be enforced within 20 years, but that period may be shortened by the time limitations of the applicable probate laws where the judgment debtor dies in the interim. Judgment debts must be filed in the same manner as other claims against the estate of a decedent.

145

Judgments and Decrees is an immensely broad subject and volumes have been written on it. Consult your local attorney if you need more specific, detailed information about the subject.

COLLECTING JUDGMENTS

Q. *I recently went to Small Claims Court and won a judgment. Now the defendant refuses to pay the judgment. What should I do?*

A. Often, obtaining the judgment is the easy part of the lawsuit. Once you have a judgment and the defendant refuses to pay, you should consider one of the following options:

1. The judgment should be recorded as it then becomes a lien on any real property that the debtor/defendant owns. If the debtor/defendant owns land in another county, you should obtain a certified copy of the judgment and record it in that county. This judgment serves as a lien on the property and has to be satisfied before clear title can be passed by the debtor to another party.

2. To find out if the debtor/defendant owns a motor vehicle, you can write to the Department of Highway Safety and Motor Vehicles, 107, Gaines Street, Tallahassee, FL 32304. The local tag office can tell you if the debtor owns a motor vehicle that is registered in the county.

3. Also available is the "deposition in aid of execution." This is a method whereby a debtor is placed under oath and asked questions about his assets before a court reporter. A subpoena is served on the debtor and can request the debtor to bring financial records, deeds, banking accounts, etc.

4. A writ of execution may also be obtained. This writ of execution is issued by the court upon the request of the creditor and allows the sheriff to take, advertise, and sell to the highest bidder enough personal property of the debtor to pay off (satisfy) the judgment and the costs of seizure, advertising and sale. The sheriff may do this until the entire judgment is paid. The writ must describe the property and must be property owned by the debtor.

5. Garnishment may also be available to collect the judgment. This is a procedure to take property of the debtor that is in the hands of a third party. This is a more complicated procedure than the other methods of collection and a court hearing is necessary.

Once you have your judgment, don't give up. Too many people get their judgment and then give up without ever getting paid. The case is not over until the debtor pays.

MISCELLANEOUS

HURRICANE POLICE POWERS

Q. *What power and authority do government and police officials have during emergencies such as hurricanes?*

A. Florida has enacted what is known as the "State Emergency Management Act" and is also referred to as Chapter 252 of the Florida Statutes. One of the emergency management powers of the governor is to:

> "Direct and compel the evacuation of all or part of the population from any stricken or threatened area within the state if he deems this action necessary for the preservation of life or other emergency mitigation, response or recovery."

The governor can also control ingress and egress of an emergency area, the movement of persons within the area and the occupancy of premises therein.

To insure that each political subdivision has the same emergency power the "Act" directs that each political subdivision is authorized and directed to establish and maintain an emergency management agency in support of the state comprehensive emergency plan and program. This literally means that political subdivisions have the same power to evacuate, prescribe modes of transportation, control ingress and egress, and even control or limit the sale of alcoholic beverages. The "Act" also provides for the provisions for the availability and use of temporary emergency housing. The legislature has provided that the state shall always have funds available to meet emergency requirements which may arise.

The penalty for any person violating any provision of the "State Emergency Management Act" is guilty of a misdemeanor of the second degree. Second degree misdemeanors are punishable with a maximum fine of $500.00 and a maximum jail sentence of 60 days.

The "Act's" main purpose is to preserve the lives and property of the citizens of the state.

GAMBLING

Q. *Please explain some of the Florida laws regarding gambling.*

A. Gambling is illegal in the state of Florida per Florida Statute Sec. 849.08. The only exception to the gambling statutes for charitable and non-profit organizations relates to bingo, and the new state lottery games.

Bingo games can be conducted legally, although there are numerous restrictions as to where, when and how this may be done. One should not try to run a bingo parlor without first seeking competent legal advice. Gambling can be legal if play money is used. The winner, however, must receive nothing of value. If anything of value is received at any time as a result of the activity, then it would be an illegal event. If donations are required in an activity rather than volunteered, it could also be construed to be gambling. If people are generally permitted to play for free, it is legal. It is a common concept that "it must be legal—everybody does it." Unfortunately, "everybody does it" will not hold up as a valid defense in a case if someone is charged with gambling.

Some events such as a billiard tournament or a bowling tournament with an entry fee and prizes for winners are legal. The law in Florida distinguishes between a game of chance and a game of skill.

Florida gambling laws also pertain to lotteries. The Supreme Court of the United States recognized many years ago that lotteries historically have been used as a means of raising funds for public purposes. Nevertheless, the Court went on to state that other "forms of gambling are comparatively innocuous when placed in contrast with the widespread use of lotteries." Lotteries have been said to prey upon the hard-earnings of the poor and the plundered, the ignorant and the simple. Lotteries are forbidden by Florida law, Florida Statute Sec. 849.09. The penalties which can be imposed for gambling violations include substantial fines, forfeitures, jail terms, problems with liquor licenses and other necessary and similar unpleasantries.

Some clubs or individuals have come across the idea to charge people an exorbitant admission fee, which includes a soft drink and a meal, and then claim that the gambling activities are free. If it can be proven that the people are paying for the privilege of participating in the gambling activities, then the club or individual will then be guilty of gambling in the state of Florida.

FRAUD

Q. *What constitutes "Fraud" and what remedies does one have if he has been a victim of fraud in the State of Florida?*

A. Fraud does not have a precise definition and the courts do not limit the "scope" of fraud. Different types of fraud are as follows:

ACTUAL FRAUD—involves an intentional truth between the parties to a transaction and generally involves misrepresentations, concealments, or other means employed to deceive in transactions.

CONSTRUCTIVE FRAUD—can best be explained by giving an example. When one has a duty in a fiduciary or confidential relationship and that duty has been abused or one takes an unconscionable advantage over another in a transaction, then "constructive fraud" has taken place.

DECEIT—actually refers to fraud as it relates to deception by misrepresentation, concealment or other contrivances.

Fraud, of course, extends to such items as contracts, deeds, real estate transactions and the sale of personal property.

STATEMENTS WHICH ARE NOT GENERALLY "FRAUD"

OPINIONS—A statement which amounts to a mere opinion, belief, or estimate generally cannot be the basis for an action in fraud. This is true even though the statement can be shown to be false. Persons relying on an "expert" opinion may have a cause of action outside this rule.

"PUFFING"—Sales talk or boasting or one who is "crying his own wares" cannot generally be proven guilty of fraud particularly when the opposite party has an equal opportunity of investigation.

STATEMENT OF FUTURE PERFORMANCE—Statements of expectation generally may not be the grounds for a proper allegation of fraud. Even if representations are made to induce others to enter into transactions, the promise to do something in the future is ordinarily not actionable fraud. Some examples of this are a corporation's capacity to produce in the future, verbal representations that contracts would be assigned to one with substantial assets, etc. Of course, if fraudulent promises were intentionally made to induce a transaction or if a promise was purposefully made with no intention to keep it, then this may be actionable.

The remedies that one has as a victim of fraud are quite involved and complex and it is recommended that if one is a victim of fraud or deceit that he engage the services of a competent attorney to discuss his remedies. Remedies will vary greatly from case to case as one remedy may be to rescind a contract and return the individuals to their original starting point, and in other cases the only remedy may be one of "damages."

GARNISHMENT

Q. *Is garnishment constitutional and can a person holding a judgment garnish a bank account?*

A. Pre-judgment garnishments have been found to be unconstitutional if:

1. No notice was provided to debtor;
2. If Writ of Garnishment is attempted without an unsworn Motion of plaintiff;
3. If debtor is not given ample opportunity to challenge the Writ.

Generally speaking, all garnishment proceedings must be specifically and strictly complied with. If the garnishment is sought before judgment, it is necessary for the plaintiff to file a motion stating that the debt or obligation is just, due and unpaid, and that the garnishment being sought is not to injure the defendant/garnishee and the defendant does not have visible property upon which a levy could have been placed. The motion should also allege that the money or other things sought are not exempt from attachment or garnishment and the attachment is not due for personal labor or services from the head of a household.

DEBTOR WITH JUDGMENT:

A person with a judgment can have a garnishment writ served on the debtor's bank. This is a very effective method of collecting a debt because it can freeze a person's money in *all* of his accounts in that bank for a period of time forcing the bank to return checks written by the debtor until the garnishment is cleaned.

The bank is required to answer the writ of garnishment by reporting and retaining any deposits within its control upon receiving the writ. The bank may deny that it holds any money relating to the writ.

GARNISHMENT OF WAGES:

Garnishment of a debtor's wages if the debtor has a judgment against him is constitutional without notice and no hearing is necessary.

GARNISHMENT OR ATTACHMENT BONDS:

Garnishment or attachment bonds are often required, and in some cases the amount must be at least double the debt or sum demanded by the plaintiff. Such bonds protect the debtor from improper tactics of persons seeking the garnishment. If interest is sought, then the bond has to be for double the interest also or it may not be effective.

DAMAGES:

The plaintiff may recover damages that were a natural and probable result of the suit if the attachment or garnishment was wrongfully or maliciously pursued. Attorney fees may also be awarded if the action was wrongfully pursued.

FICTITIOUS NAMES & MAIDEN NAMES

Q. *Please explain what is required to file a name under the Fictitious Name Statute.*

A. Under the "Fictitious Name Statute" it is unlawful for any person to engage in business under a fictitious name unless it is registered, as required by the Florida Statute. The definition of the word "person" includes every individual, whether natural or artificial, firm or group or combination of individuals or partnerships, whether natural or representative.

The purpose of the Statute is to provide notice to the public so that anyone operating under a fictitious name can be notified by any other party and the real party would be registered at the county court house.

A notice of intent to use a fictitious name must be published in a designated county newspaper at least once a week for four consecutive weeks before the petitioner (or person desiring to use the name) is allowed to register the name with the clerk of the circuit court where the business will take place.

The filing of the name with the clerk must include the names and addresses of all the parties involved in the business, and the extent of their interest in the business.

Certain types of individuals such as physicians, dentists, podiatrists, chiropractors, naturopaths, and osteopaths are expressly prohibited from practicing under any name but their own. Certified public accountants, partnerships or corporations also may not practice under any names that are misleading or deceptive, but are allowed to practice under fictitious names that are not misleading or deceptive to the public.

Any of the above if found guilty of using a different name for their business (in the case of physicians, etc.) or if any CPA, partnership or corporation is found guilty of using a misleading fictitious name, may have their license suspended or revoked. Legal sanctions are similarly imposed upon any person who falsely impersonates any of the above mentioned parties.

In the case of noncompliance with the provisions of the Statute, neither the business nor the owner of the business may defend or maintain a lawsuit until compliance of all the requirements mentioned above. If one is found guilty of violating the Statute, he could be fined or sentenced to jail.

Q. *I recently married and want to know if I can keep my maiden name?*

A. Yes. Nothing prohibits you from maintaining your maiden name as your legal name even though the marital relationship continues. In fact, if you so choose to maintain your maiden name, the Department of Highway Safety and Motor Vehicles must process your application for a drivers license in your maiden name.

MECHANICS LIENS

Q. *Could you explain mechanics liens?*

A. The Supreme Court of Florida has stated that the fundamental purpose of the mechanics lien law is ". . . to protect those whose materials and skills improve the land of others by providing a plan by which such persons or firms may receive their fair share of the moneys payable by the owner to the general contractor under the direct contract or, in circumstances specified by the statute may rescind and foreclose a claim of lien against the property so improved."

Generally, those who contribute to the permanent improvement of the real estate may use this vehicle including architects, landscape architects, engineers and land surveyors who have performed services in the preparation of plans, specifications or drawings are included and their liens extend to the property in connection with which their services are performed, regardless of whether the planned improvements are actually are constructed. Parties furnishing plants that are planted on property and those furnishing carpets that are permanently affixed also may specifically use liens.

Various property may be exempt from liens. If the contract price is no more than $500.00 and is completed within six months from actual commencement the property may not be exempt from mechanics liens. However, if an owner requires his contractor to furnish a payment bond, as provided in Florida Code, this exempts the property from liens under the act, except for the lien of the Contractor furnishing the bond.

Any party having an interest in real property may relieve the property of a claim of lien filed against it by transferring that lien to a cash deposit or surety bond.

Claims of lien from the contractor are generally required to be filed not later than 90 days after the final furnishing of the labor or services or materials by the lienor. Failure to serve a copy of the claim of lien within ten days after claim has been recorded renders the claim of lien voidable.

Also, it is a requirement that notice to the owner be given not later than 45 days after the commencement of the furnishing of services or materials.

There are many considerations involved in mechanics liens and each case should be discussed with a competent attorney before any action is taken.

DRUNK DRIVING

Q. *What penalties are involved with drunk-driving charges?*

A. Formerly the driving-while-intoxicated (DWI) law required first offenders to pay a fine not to exceed $500.00, give up their licenses for 90 days and pay $78.00 to take a substance abuse course before getting back their driving privileges.

Now, if a judge or jury finds a person guilty of DWI, the offender will lose his license up to 1 year, pay a minimum fine of $250.00, perform 50 hours of community service and possibly serve up to 6 months in jail.

The second offense will result in a minimum penalty jump to $500.00 and ten days in jail and a license suspension of up to five years, (if convicted within 3 years from 1st offense).

The third offense carries with it a ten-year license suspension, $1,000.00 fine and minimum 30 days in jail up to 1 year in jail.

Under the new law, effective July 1, 1982, a first offender must attend and complete drunk drivers school to obtain a court permit to drive to and from work.

Q. *Must drivers perform roadside sobriety tests that are requested by police?*

A. No, but . . .

1. A driver that refuses to take the test may lose his license for 90 days;
2. Refusal to take the test is admissable as evidence against the driver in court;
3. A police officer who has reasonable cause to believe the driver has caused death or injury can require a blood sample to be taken.

Q. *Can a driver request the sobriety test?*

A. Yes. If the officer believes the driver is intoxicated, the driver may demand to take a pre-arrest breathalyzer test, which reflects the amount of alcohol in his blood. Such a test is not admissable against him in a trial.

Q. *May the police demand breath tests after the arrest?*

A. No. A driver may refuse to submit to breath, urine, and blood samples tests for alcohol and drugs.

Q. *How should I respond to questions from an officer if stopped for drunk driving?*

A. Anything you do and say can be used against you in a court of law. Generally drivers talk too much, take tests they could refuse, and build a case against themselves. The best advice I can give is not to mix drinking with driving.

SEXUAL HARASSMENT

Q. *Please explain the recent developments in sexual harassment suits and what legal remedies are available.*

A. Sexual harassment and discrimination has received widespread attention and has been an area that has recently exploded with many legal changes and remedies. Perhaps the reason for the growth in this area of the law is the "titillating" quality of the facts of the cases and the "tabloid" effect the cases show as they appeal very much to the public's curiosity.

Another reason for the recent interest is the amount of the verdicts due to many state courts awarding punitive damages with the added charges of assault, battery, intentional infliction of emotional distress and slander. In Federal Court the remedies are somewhat restricted under Title VII, 42 U.S.C. et seq.

STATE GOVERNMENT ORDER

Governor Bob Graham of Florida, signed an Executive Order 81-69 on June 25, 1981, preventing any sexual harassment in the State Government. Its purpose was to provide a work atmosphere free from sexual harassment.

ELEMENTS OF SEXUAL HARASSMENT

Sexual Harassment can be proven when requests for sexual favors, unwelcomed sexual advances and other verbal or physical conduct can be based on the following factors: (a) Submission to conduct made explicitly or implicitly on the threat or condition of employment; (b) Rejection or submission based on sexual favors or absence of sexual favors which determine employment opportunities or hiring practices; or (c) conduct which unreasonably interferes with an individual's work performance or creating an intimidating, hostile or offensive working environment.

In determining whether alleged conduct constitutes sexual harassment the courts will look at past practices, the company's history, employment patterns, the totality of the circumstances of the sexual advance. Determinations in court are based on a case-by-case method and the law is still emerging in this field.

Employers are responsible for conduct of employees in the workplace where they *should have known* of the conduct unless they can show they took immediate and corrective action.

If employment opportunities, benefits or promotions are based on sexual reasons, then a sexual discrimination charge can be raised. Sexual discrimination charges are usually devastating to the careers of both the plaintiff and defendant. The defense of "encouragement and sexy dress" and actions and submission are almost always used. One recent case was won by the defendant because the parties had had a love affair for a year and a half. The court found that discrimination or harassment did not exist.

The goal of the court is to return the person to "whole" which is nearly impossible, thus large verdicts are generally the rule in successful cases.

BAKER ACT

Q. *What emergency provisions are provided by Florida Law to commit an individual to a mental hospital?*

A. Under the "Baker Act" or "The Florida Mental Health Act" an individual may be admitted to a mental hospital or other such facility on emergency conditions if he is believed to be mentally ill and because of such illness is likely to physically injure himself or others if he is not immediately detained. Emergency admissions are initiated in any of the following three manners:

1. A judge may sign an order (ex parte) which states that from the facts presented to the court that the individual in question must be taken to a receiving facility for emergency examination and treatment. The order of the court shall be made a part of the patient's record and the judge, of course, must be convinced beyond a reasonable doubt that such action is necessary; or

2. If a law enforcement officer has reason to believe that an individual is mentally ill and because of such illness, is likely to physically injure himself or others if he is not immediately detained, such officer may take that individual into custody and to the nearest receiving facility for emergency examination and treatment. The officer has a duty to execute a written report detailing the circumstances as to why the individual was thought to be mentally ill, or of a danger to himself or others, and said report shall be a part of the patient's clinical record; or

3. A physician may execute a certificate stating that he has examined an individual within the preceding 48 hours and according to his observations and conclusions, finds that the individual appears to meet the criteria for emergency admission. The physician's statement alone should be enough to allow a police officer to take the individual into custody as described above. The physician must also submit a detailed report which should become a part of the individual's clinical record.

It should be noted that a patient admitted under the above rules shall be examined without unnecessary delay; and if the physician concludes that the patient should not be hospitalized, he shall be released immediately (unless criminal charges, etc.). Also, any physician, law enforcement officer, attorney, health officer, or hospital officer or employee who acts in good faith is immune from civil or criminal liability for his actions in connection with the admission, diagnosis, treatment or discharge of a patient.

HOME SOLICITATION SALES

Q. *Does a buyer have a right to revoke a home solicitation sale?*

A. Yes. Under Florida Statute Section 501.021—501.055 a buyer has the right to cancel a home solicitation sale until midnight of the third business day after the day on which the buyer signs an agreement or offer to purchase. Cancellation is evidenced by the buyer giving written notice of cancellation *in person,* *by telegram,* or *by mail* to the seller at the address stated in the agreement or offer to purchase. Written notice of cancellation given by mail shall be effective upon the postmark of the letter. Only a written expression of intent to cancel is necessary and the form of the notice does not have to be written in any particular way.

A warning notice of the buyer's right to cancel must appear on all notes or other evidence of indebtedness given pursuant to any home solicitation sale. The notice usually reads as follows: "This is a home solicitation sale, and if you do not want the goods or services, you may cancel this agreement by providing written notice to the seller in person, by telegram, or by mail. This notice must indicate that you do not want the goods or services and must be delivered or postmarked before midnight of the third business day after you sign this agreement. If you cancel this agreement, the seller may keep all or part of any cash downpayment, not to exceed the lesser of 5% of the cash price or $50.00.

To qualify for a "home solicitation sale," the sale must be for at least $25.00 and occur outside the seller's main place of business. Some of the possible exceptions to this rule are as follows:

1. Arrangements made pursuant to prior negotiations in the course of a visit by buyer to seller's retail business establishment.
2. When the buyer initiates the contract and the goods are needed to meet a bona fide personal emergency and the buyer signs a warranty.
3. Sale conducted entirely by mail or telephone, and without any other contact between the buyer and seller.
4. Buyer initiated the contact and specifically requested the seller to visit his home for the purpose of maintenance.
5. Sales pertaining to the sale or rental of property, sale of insurance, or sale of securities or commodities by a registered agent.

BAILMENTS

Q. *What is a bailment?*

A. Bailments are a form of contracts where possession (not title) are transferred from one person to another. An example of a bailment would be taking your clothes to the cleaner's or leaving your automobile in a parking lot. The owner is called the bailor; the one given temporary possession is the bailee. The bailee must take reasonable care of the property, and in the absence of an agreement to the contrary, is liable for negligence, but is not generally liable for damages if he has not been negligent. For example, if you lend me your automobile and a third person negligently runs into me and damages your car without any fault on my part, I am not generally responsible for the damage done.

The main point a lay person needs to know is that the bailee (parking lot owner, or dry cleaner, etc.) owes a duty to take proper care of the article entrusted to him. A garage owner, for example, is responsible for a car entrusted to him but probably not responsible for jewelry or other items left in the car.

The bailee can attempt to limit his liability by printing disclaimers on a parking lot ticket or hanging "not responsible" signs in the area. Such tactics are not necessarily binding as the bailee cannot be negligent in his entrustment of the item. He must make a reasonable effort to safeguard property entrusted to him and to properly handle such items.

A parking lot owner usually would not be responsible for a "ding" in a door caused by another customer but would be responsible if a parking lot employee was drunk and ran your car into a cement column.

Claims of liens can arise out of bailment situations. The typical situation arises from the garage owner (the bailee) placing a lien on a car until the repair bill is paid. Such a lien is perfectly valid. Problems arise when the value of the work is disputed, however, in the case of automobiles, written quotes must be given.

Some people think a hospital has a lien on a newborn baby. This is not true. Hospitals may not hold babies as hostages until the bill is paid.

There are many situations which occur under many different circumstances. If you think a bailee has breached his duty of reasonable care, you should ask an attorney.

STATUTE OF LIMITATIONS

Q. *What time limit must I be concerned about if I am to sue someone on a breach of contract?*

A. Most "actions" have a period of time in Florida in which you must pursue your rights or you will lose your right to do so. This period of time within which you must act is called the "Statute of Limitations."

The computation of time begins from the time the action arose. A cause of action accrues when the last element constituting the cause of action occurs. In some cases the period of time starts to run when the "problem" is discovered or should have been discovered. Some of the more common problems and the statute of limitation time limit within which you must take action are as follows:

Products Liability	Within 12 years
Fraud	Within 4 years
State Tax (except where certificates sold or taxes levied under Chapter 198 and 220)	Within 5 years
Contract, Note, Liability founded on a contract	Within 5 years
Action on a Judgment	Within 20 years

Foreclose a Mortgage	Within 5 years
Rescind a Contract	Within 4 years
Libel, slander, assault, battery, false arrest, malicious prosecution	Within 4 years
Recover personal property	Within 4 years
Trespass	Within 4 years
Action relating to determination of paternity	Within 4 years
Taking, detaining or injuring personal property	Within 4 years
Professional Malpractice (other than medical)	Within 2 years
Medical Malpractice	Within 2 years

from time incident occurred or 2 years from time discovered with exercise of due diligence or no later than 4 years from date of incident

Wrongful death	Within 2 years
Wages or overtime	Within 2 years
Specific performance of contract	Within 1 year
Enforcement of bulk transfer	Within 1 year

The Statute of Limitation may be tolled (delayed) for several reasons. Generally, they are:

1. The absence of the person from the state that is being sued;
2. Use of a false name by the person being sued so that process cannot be served;
3. Concealment in the state of the person to be sued so that process cannot be served on him;
4. The person entitled to sue is declared incompetent;
5. The payment of any part of the principal or interest of an obligation.

The best advice on most occasions is not to delay but to pursue your legal rights on a timely basis. If this advice is followed, the Statute of Limitations will not be a problem.

RELEASING LIENS

Q. *A service station owner is holding my car until I pay a bill for services, the amount of which I think is unfair. What should I do?*

A. You should have received a written estimate on all repairs over $50.00. If the owner failed to provide such an estimate, he may have lost some of his rights in collecting his money.

The first problem you have is recovering your car. One method available is posting a cash bond with the clerk of the court. The amount of the bond is the same amount of the invoice. The law states that "any lienor (service station owner) who, upon posting of the bond fails to release or return the property to the lienee (you) pursuant to Section 713.76 of Florida Statutes is guilty of a misdemeanor of the second degree, punishable as provided in Sec. 775.082, Sec. 775.083 or Sec. 775.084 of Florida Statutes."

The law further states that whenever a lienee brings an action in the appropriate court with respect to any property which has been wrongfully detained by a lienor in violation of this Section (713.76), the lienee, upon a judgment in the lienee's favor, shall be entitled to damages, reasonable court costs, and attorney's fees sustained by the lienee of such wrongful detention. This procedure is available against anyone who is making repairs for you and who may be holding your personal property.

As you can see, if a service station owner is holding your car until you pay for the repair, you can post a cash bond with the clerk of the court and the station owner must release the car or be guilty of a misdemeanor, and the station owner might also be liable for attorney fees. Of course, service station owners may place liens on cars where they have performed services and eventually if they follow the proper procedure could sell the car to have the lien paid off.

Generally, in the case of a sale of a vehicle to satisfy a lien, a notice must be sent at least 45 days before the date of sale and must include, but not be limited to:

A description of the vehicle;

Name and address and phone number of owner and any other person claiming an interest;

Name, address, phone number of lienor;

Notice of lien for services;

Notice of sale and whether it is a public or private sale.

The enforcement of liens can be difficult and you should consult your attorney before proceeding to enforce a lien.

THE RULE OF 78'S

Q. *I wanted to make an early payoff of my car loan and the payoff balance was much higher than I anticipated. Please explain the "Rule of 78's"*

A. It is a common misconception to assume that all of the equal installments used to repay a loan contain the same amount of interest. Thus, a person might believe that if he repays a loan in one year instead of two years he will pay only one-half the total interest. However, the method which the lending institution chooses to calculate the sum necessary to repay the loan is the deciding factor in determining how much interest has been paid and how much principal is due.

One common way for lending institutions to compute interest is based on a mathematical formula known as the "Rule of 78's" or the "sum of the digits". The basic method of computing the interest is based on a formula which has a good portion of the interest paid in the early stage of the loan. The interest in each installment is the fraction of the number of months remaining in which the borrower must make payments, divided by the sum of the digits of the number of months in the installment plan.

For example, in a 12-month installment plan, the sum of the numbers 1 through 12 is 78 $(1 + 2 + 3 + 4 + 5 + 6 + 7 + 8 + 9 + 10 + 11 + 12 = 78)$. Under the rule of 78's the first month's interest payment would be 12/78's of the total interest; the second month's interest payment would be 11/78's, etc. until the last month's would be 1/78 of the total interest. As you can see, most of the interest is paid early in the loan period and only a very small percentage is paid toward the end.

It should be noted that if a buyer was attracted to a low rate of interest under the "rule of 78's" and paid the loan off early, he would actually be paying a much higher rate of interest than he intended.

Some lending institutions offer "normal" loans to their preferred customers rather than requiring them to buy a car under the "rule of 78's". The advantage, of course, is that you can pay off early with no penalty, or you can refinance with no penalty. The "rule of 78's" actually has a penalty for refinancing or early payoff.

If your car dealership offers to secure financing from a local bank with a good rate, be sure to inquire as to the type of financing. It is customary for the "rule of 78's" to be in the fine print on the back of the contract. It should also be noted that this type of financing is common on other types of installment sales.

This article is not to imply that the "rule of 78's" is bad but only to inform you of the different types of financing in which you may already be involved.

CAR OWNERSHIP

Q. *Should a husband and wife own a car jointly or in one name?*

A. The name in which a vehicle is registered needs careful consideration because most states hold that the owner could be liable as well as the driver for damages which are negligently caused. If the damage caused exceeds the liability insurance, the owner's and/or the driver's assets may be attached. Thus, if you are married and own most of your assets jointly, your automobile should probably be registered in your individual name. In this way only the driver's assets held individually will be vulnerable in case of a catastrophic accident. Jointly held assets would be protected.

Married couples who own two vehicles should probably each have the vehicle they drive most frequently registered in their own name.

Of course, there are other considerations in deciding which name to register a car. There are tax considerations for cars used in business and for the owner to obtain the maximum tax advantages, the car might have to be in the name of the business. Many firms which own one or more vehicles have decided to incorporate to avoid some of the potential liabilities of car ownership.

Probate is always a concern in deciding vehicle ownership. Married people feel that joint ownership is an easy method in which to own a car and thus will avoid probate. This precaution is unnecessary because most states provide a simple procedure after death to transfer the car to the surviving spouse without a formal probate proceeding. This can be accomplished for a very nominal fee.

Registering your child's car in your name can be very risky. Although it may reduce the insurance premiums for your child, the consequences and liabilities can be devastating if the child has an accident and especially if the child has a bad driving record.

Owning your car in a Living Trust is also not generally advisable. If the owner of your car is yourself as Trustee, then you have broadcasted that you have a Trust which possibly owns other assets. Since you and your Trust are considered the same person, there is no protection against a law suit being filed against the owner (you, the Trustee). Thus, the Trust does not serve as a "credit or liability shelter." As previously indicated, cars are not difficult to probate between husband and wife.

Finally, changing the ownership from husband and wife to one or the other is a simple procedure. The reverse side of the car title is filled out, signed, notarized and taken to Department of Motor Vehicles for the issuance of a new title.

MEDICARE

Q. *What information can you provide me about Medicare?*

A. Blue Shield of Florida handles Medicare payments for the United States Government. Their address is: P.O. Box 2525, Jacksonville, FL 32231.
Phone No. 1-800-342-7586

Information is available at any Social Security Administration Office.

Disputes are handled by the Insurance Commissioner located at The Capitol, Tallahassee, FL 32301.

Q. *Can I obtain supplemental medical insurance policies in addition to Medicare?*

A. Yes. Many companies carry supplemental policies. These policies do not generally cover nursing home expense or custodial care. Medicare does pay for impatient care after you have been in a hospital if your condition requires rehabilitation services or a skilled nurse for your recovery.

Q. *Do doctors accept Medicare's payment as payment in full?*

A. Different doctors have different methods of payment. You should ask your doctor if he will accept Medicare payments as full payment; many will.

Q. *What is Medicaid?*

A. Medicaid is for low income persons and acts as supplemental insurance to Medicare. Your eligibility will depend on your financial situation and physical condition.

Q. *Who is eligible for Medicare hospital insurance at age 65?*

A. Generally, you are eligible if:

1. You receive monthly Social Security or Railroad Retirement benefits;
2. You have worked long enough to be insured under Social Security or Railroad Retirement system;
3. You have worked long enough in federal employment to be insured for Medicare;
4. You may be eligible if you are a widow or widower, divorced to someone eligible, or dependent parents.

Q. *Can you be eligible for Medicare before age 65?*

A. Yes. You may be eligible if:

1. You have been entitled to Social Security disability for 24 months;
2. You have worked sufficient time in federal employment and meet the requirements of Social Security disability program;
3. You are a disabled widow or widower, disabled surviving divorced spouse, and disabled children 18 years of age or older may be eligible;
4. You need maintenance dialysis or a kidney transplant for permanent kidney failure, and you are insured or getting monthly benefits.

Q. *Can I obtain Medicare if I continue to work past age 65 and have not applied for Social Security benefits?*

A. Yes, but you have to file an application to receive the benefits.

For additional copies of the book, ASK AN ATTORNEY, send $12.95 to P.O. Box 10005, Largo, FL 33543.

Enclosed please find $_____ for _____ copies of ASK AN ATTOR-NEY.

Send to:

Name _____

Address _____

City _____ State _____ Zip _____